Holding On
To Me
In Lockdown

Mike Ferguson

PublishNation
www.publishnation.co.uk

For Karis, Ana, Val

With my thanks to Chris for his encouraging support and
astute help in seeing this memoir to its completion

Covid Lockdown Memoirs

Everyone and their proverbial has written a lockdown memoir and I tend to be interested in those by musicians, though haven't read any yet in being too busy writing mine. I know about releases from Richard Thompson and Rickie Lee Jones, so that's good if competitive company, but how do you contest with someone like Thompson whose lifetime career was/is so full he felt he could reminisce on his beginnings with Fairport Convention in 1967 and then end the book mid-1970s? Jones could have written a substantial account based wholly on her relationship with Tom Waits. As for the modster Paul Weller – in an *Observer* review[1] about him and his music, he talks of having been asked many times to write a memoir but has persistently declined, explaining 'Nah. People always ask me to write my memoirs…No. I'm going to do another book…which is not a biography at all, but me just talking about my life and childhood and all that stuff…' so, perhaps the competition for knowing what *is* and writing a memoir isn't as fierce as I imagine. A tester on the proliferation of books in this genre is when you type into a search engine *everyone has a story to tell* and get fed a glut of related quotes – most from people you've never heard of before. Nevertheless, I was compelled to write mine, and here it is about all kinds of stuff.

---

[1] *The Observer – the new review* 14.3.21

Omaha

Having retired – plus lockdown – there was plenty of time to think and do, so I made a virtual trip back to the town of my birth using Google Maps, its visual of my former duplex home on North 40th a surprise in its neglected state, though after all these years I shouldn't be surprised. There is also the innate corrective to any imagined sustained joy of that time: no enduring recalls of happiness stand out where sitting on the concrete front porch – still there – to watch cars drive past is a lonely vignette of the days also drifting by, and the corner bakery seems long gone, frustrating a sentimental and pictorial aide-mémoire of occasional childhood eating pleasures. As an external view, a smorgasbord Christmas in the front room is yet more unreachable, and seeing the fenced-off back yard where a car had flattened my pet garter snake doesn't answer how it had escaped there, assuming I'd not left it to slither around unattended. It is on the corner at Hamilton Street where I feel most cheated in the visiting, unsure which of the shops used to be Martin's Donuts, only assuming it directly on the bend where as a six-year-old I'd pulled my red wagon part-filled with toys to panhandle for the price of a chocolate topped ring.

Duplex on North 40th, Omaha

Teaching Creative Writing

Focusing on creative writing was always the great pleasure as an English teacher, especially with experimental poetry: concrete, cut-up, humuments. However, I have on occasions made mistakes with some exemplar and resources. There was the *Beheadings* – not my idea – with model poems by Miroslav Holub where removing the first letter of a word leaves another (p/ear) and you create poetic riddles from this process. That title needed a change, especially for younger writers, so I went for the comparative etymological logic of a horticulture term *Deadheadings*, pleased with added humour in the 'tag' line *Is a Deadheaded Sunflower an Unflower?* More seriously problematic though was in my GCSE poetry textbook by a large national publisher from 1999 where I wanted to engage students through the broadest themes so included an extract from a Timothy Emlyn Jones' football poem – this visually moving all over the page like a game, with much about 'pass / pass / pass' and 'come up / come up on the outside' and 'easy / ease the ball' and so on as a mimetic account of playing football. I had a change of perspective years later when I revisited and had an instant feeling of nausea whilst reading the following 'come / come / come my darling' and another which I'd originally thought a beautiful lyrical line 'an arc of grace sprung high' making me suddenly aware it was a detailed, erotic poem about fornicating and ejaculation – another physical clue being the darling's (*darling* FFS!) 'toe it turn / ease the moment'.

When I Met Derrida

I had sent my poem about Jacques Derrida titled *Derr ida Derr i da* to the 'Times Literary Supplement' with what I thought a concise definition of deconstruction, but there was, paradoxically, no room for an alternative reading in their rejection of this, an ending to that hopefulness like the word *caboose* which closed the poem. This would have been in 1980, a year after meeting him, receiving an invitation to attend a private talk he was giving at one of the Oxford colleges. Ann Wordsworth, my tutor then, had arranged this, a thank you for my immersion in her wonderful teaching, drinking red wine at her house when reading essays aloud on, for example, Lawrence's non-frictional sex proclivities and other Freudian impressions. Derrida's talk was well-attended, though the only person I recognised was the literary critic Maud Ellman, and Derrida held the reverential audience of that room for over an hour, if not more, and I hadn't expected to meet him personally, but he spoke to me as I was leaving, considerate pleasantries I would guess, and it embarrasses me still – though I can also laugh – how awkward and diffident I was, probably appearing rather rude, in ignoring everything he said. This was because I couldn't understand a word he spoke, just like his entire talk, my not speaking any French, though perhaps I might have expected him to.

That Grifter Time

It was reading about Lilly Dillon's racetrack scam in Jim Thompson's *The Grifters* that reminded me I'd done something similar in the 70s with Chris (a temporary lecturer at my civic college) enticing me to be his accomplice because I seemed like someone willing to take a risk, or the fact I was an American too. In his best *film noire* visualisation, he'd explained what would happen to him if the criminal gang conveying the Tote information on racing days found out he was subsequently sharing this with me. Their cheat wasn't unlawful, just a national racket abusing a system, though me placing bets aged 17 was illegal. Well into this shadowing job, the bookies didn't always take my wagers on the horses, sometimes because they'd heard on the wind about a con happening in their town – we varied this place every so often – or because my £30 flutters at a time rang suspicion bells: a lot of money in 1972 *and* from a hippie who looked like one. The jeopardy was, however, all with my duplicitous college lecturer, and at £5 a session for me that was a lot of easy-enough cider money. The day of the one massive win was memorable. Chris had been somewhere else in town and when I saw him coming towards me in the street at the end of our business, his face was beaming. It didn't make sense though as I hadn't placed any winning personal bet for him that day, misreading the notes Chris had given and only learning about this miserable error when he explained with all that terrible and dreadful disappointment a teacher can sometimes have in a student.

The Beatles in Iowa in 1964

'How they startled in clean-cut suits and ties – / those harmonies as pure as Country and Western or hymns' are reconciling lines for the incongruity of seeing the Beatles in Elk Horn Iowa in '64. They are from my poem published with other poetic tributes by actual well-known writers in the *Newspaper Taxis* fab four anthology of 2013. I could as easily have contributed to a Beach Boys collection having written an ode to *Surfer Girl* from '63 with its offering of distant beaches and custom cars. Of course, *She Loves You* came via Ed Sullivan's ironic mainline into all-American homes providing alternative hope in its possible make-believe of complete difference, the Beatles being exotic because they were English – rather than hot rods anyone anywhere in the USA could see but not necessarily have. But a moptop was easy to grow beyond a flattop: if you could brave the hatred, as I had to six years later in Michigan when getting death threats for being 'that guy with long hair'. I'd also written about Quang Duc turning himself into a fireball, though that too was much later as a composition, and though this hadn't come through loud and clear when it happened, we practised surviving a nuclear attack by crouching under our school desks with hands over heads to prepare for that knife-edge of the Cuban missile crisis. Not all hopeful innocence then, like the cruel small-town things we did with cherry bombs, and I do regret sharing this vivid detail in my later teaching about how to structure a compelling descriptive narrative.

Deferred

I knew I wouldn't have to fight in the Vietnam War when my Selective Service notification of *Class 1 – H* arrived at Belstead in November 1972 and explained 'Registrant not currently subject to processing for induction'. Years later when teaching, I was involved in making a couple of short GCSE educational videos, one about the poem *What Were They Like?* by Denise Levertov. We filmed two alternative readings of the poem with a small group of students and my role was as a teacher who happened to be an American, living in the UK, and who could have been sent to fight in that war. All fine and good, apart from the tedious length of my narrative constructed from what appeared a seamless sequence of varied head shots – these disguising the many edits needed to stop and restart because of my recurring errors. But I was able to show my 'Notice of Classification' papers as well as a passport photo of me from the time with long hippie hair, establishing all of the clichéd credentials for my being anti-war, rather than simply scared. The other video was where I provided readings for Lawrence Ferlinghetti's poem *Two Scavengers in a Truck, Two Beautiful People in a Mercedes,* one dressed as the garbage man and the other as a flash business executive. Sometime after this, one of the students at my school stopped me in a corridor to tell me he'd been watching a film on BBC2 late at night, drinking quite a bit of alcohol and subsequently falling asleep in his chair with the TV left turned on. He then described his horror in waking at 3 or 4 in the morning with me in his living room wearing a black sleeveless vest and talking about things he couldn't understand. It turns out BBC2 aired its *Bitesize* GCSE education programmes in the early dead-time hours of TV scheduling, these featuring the short poetry films, presumably on a repeating cycle and obviously for teachers and/or students to have set for recording.

Ruskin College

Attending a civic college to study A-levels, I was happy for having a place to be back in my UK home, escaping the small town near Flint, Michigan where my life had been threatened. English was my favourite subject, being an aspiring writer; Geography was a filler and I was dismissed from this for misbehaviour on a field trip to Buxton Gorge, and my third of Economic and Social History was taught by two Communists. I revelled in the radical take on the Poor Laws and Enclosure, not that these needed any finessing to the Left, and was surprisingly interested in learning about the historical significance of Stevenson's *Rocket*. I will never forget and always appreciate the experience of a two-day event a friend and I attended at Ruskin College, Oxford with our pair of teachers. We'd been asked/selected for our clear radical sensibilities, and though I cannot recall any of the lectures that weekend, I have the fondest memories of nights drinking pints of ale and sharing bread and cheese meals, communing with the more adult attendees who sang and played folk songs of proletarian injustices as well as protest and revolution I felt increasingly prepared to incite whenever getting the call. I failed my A-level, but on retaking, managed a grade D. I did achieve an A for English – my best exam essay, I suspect, being a response to a question about the exchange of letters between Dorothea and Casaubon in *Middlemarch,* genuinely the only part of that ridiculously huge exam tome I had read.

And I Used to Sell Brass Rubbings

Deciding in 1972 to become an entrepreneur and support my writing career, I set up the *Medieval Art Studio* business with John who was taking a break from studying for a PhD in Theology. He produced the rubbings and I wrote sales-pitch letters to American department stores on stationery designed by a friend with an actual job. When Sears and Roebuck didn't even acknowledge my terms for providing sole access to these genuine 'antiquities', John gave up on me and the *MAS*, leaving quite a bit of the stock at my cottage, and disappeared. I got a job working on a local farm to earn my first regular wage, and a couple of years later flew to the States with my girlfriend to visit my family who then lived in Lexington Kentucky, taking a large tube of rolled-up brass rubbings with us. I had two unforgettable experiences while there: the first was seeing a Ku Klux Klan rally from a Greyhound bus window as we passed, though inexplicably I cannot recall any details whatsoever; and second was when I took the rubbings into various small-town American antique shops near Lexington and, putting on my best English accent, spun tales about their origins and the art of capturing monumental brasses on paper, selling almost all I had brought with me. In 1994 I won first prize in the Sidmouth Arts Festival Open Entry Poetry Competition with my poem about the Ku Klux Klan encounter titled *I See the Want to in Your Eyes*, this itself the name of a Conway Twitty song actually about love for his partner, but that relates to a whole other contextualising.

Grandpa Telling a Lie

Grandpa slept alone in the broad attic room of his Elk Horn home and I would follow, listening, his slow heavy steps up the turning stairs. Grandma, having unturned her extraordinarily long hair from its bun, would be reading a bedtime story in hers on the ground floor whenever I stayed. During the day, Grandpa would sit on the outdoor porch talking with his pet bee, or in that front room riding the rocker's run, plug ringing in a spittoon with cigar smoke later on his breath or being blown into my ear to banish an ache away. He would clearly have been aware that I stole a dollar bill from his wallet, and the curfew he'd set for my being home was not a punishment but because he would always know, and when that driver rode up in his car and stopped with the window down – drying mud on the side of his angry face – Grandpa didn't need to see my dirtied hands to warn the man how the day had been very hot and it was time to be on his way.

With Grandpa and Grandma Carlson, visiting Omaha,
March 1957

Near Flint and the Redneck Centre of the Universe

Having left England in 1970, unsure if I would return, I spent a couple of months back in the States, mainly with my older sister Melanie and her family near Flint in Michigan, and then briefly in Oakland Iowa with just my parents and other two sisters before flying back to Suffolk for continuing my education, desperate to escape a now alien America. My brother-in-law Bill in that redneck part of Michigan was ex-Army, a big guy, and not someone to mess with, yet even on the day we made tie-dye T-shirts to wear that night at a local stock car race, the battle of the culture wars began. With both of us standing for the *Star-Spangled Banner,* I heard that first abuse directed my way and got this intimidation continued later in the toilets as well as having empty beer cans thrown at me when leaving the track. A comfort and a catharsis could be found with family, yet in an alternative elemental way, I got extra of the latter feeling as payback when being driven about in one of Bill's sassy cars or his custom motorbike. We had fast smooth glides up roads in the Thunderbird, and then gutsier, throaty propulsions in his Coventry TR4, tuned specially for fuckyou over-takings. On impulse one balmy night, we headed off on the bike for Canada – just for the hell of it and my never having been there – but on nearing the border (the title of my first collection of poems), we turned around and headed back home.

Rose of Sharon at Belstead Cottage

When compiling a personal dictionary of 'interesting' words for use in my writing, I was still mistaking the Black Mountain poets' actual education for intentional, impressive complexities, and composed much of my wordy tonnage of latter teens/early 20s poetry in late night flurries living then in my Belstead home. The landlords Maud and Arthur Brown had somehow acquired enough money working all their respective lives as a cook and a farm horseman to buy the single L-shaped block of five formerly tied cottages from William Paul & Sons. I managed to start renting mine, still at college aged 17, with my parents in the States agreeing to pay the fee, an important guarantee for this first letting. There was no indoor toilet or hot water in mine or any of the others, so it was a basic but beautiful place and each room was unusually small, or as would be romantically described, *quaint.* There was a downstairs living area with fireplace, a tiny closet, slightly larger-than-minute kitchen with cold-tap in a mini sink, and Belling cooker with solo ring and a Fray Bentos pie-size oven; upstairs was the one nearly ordinary sized bedroom with a genuine brass bed (and pottery mattress warmers) and then again a much smaller second bedroom at its side: this the room where I was reading and arriving at that last chapter of *Grapes of Wrath* – Rose of Sharon's gesture of humanity a profound, memorable finale to a teenager's couple of weeks reading all of Steinbeck's novels.

What I Miss

Reflecting on personal history so far back and intensively, you are prompted to consider what is missed in other times, not as much in youth – all those dramas of growing up – but in comparing the here and now with a more recent past, relatively speaking. While these days I'm on the computer all of the time – emails, blogging, social media; searching fake and real news, where that next missile will land, the absurd words on how to stop it all – it is thirty odd years ago that I miss (if shocked to call this *more recent*): queuing outside for sausages, the butcher baiting me about teachers' holidays; queueing outside again for bread, fresh smells wafting down the long line; bottled milk each day on the step at the front gate, and therefore seeing Bill – old Luxton – at his shop in town to pay the account, tallying in a notebook with a pencil, adding up what was owed in real numbers.

No Win No Fee

An insentient late Christmas Eve of 1971 rolled into Christmas Day, though I woke then for a few more aware days in hospital. My good friend Lawrence would race me everywhere I wanted to go on his motorbike, so I was a regular pillion passenger urging him on, and when we hit the dislodged manhole cover in the road it was no one else's fault but the local highway maintenance department. Lawrence was fine, but my helmet face-visor had cracked open over my nose, not severing it but leaving a gash needing stitches, and I was picked up unconscious by the ambulance – that helmet having saved my life. In hospital later I was most desperate to write a note and send with a poem to the girl I had very recently met, expressing my situation, that I was alright, and including some poetically romantic yearnings – and she did visit, more out of curiosity than anything. As I reflect back on the 'accident', I do rue the fact there didn't seem then to be any *No Win No Fee* insurance claim companies who could have tackled that Ipswich highways maintenance department for me and secured a tidy compensation sum for the both of us. This said, as we near our 45th wedding anniversary, Val and I have happy memories of those days and that meeting, she having been encouraged to go and visit me when her best friend's older brother said I was an OK guy, though Val does inform and correct me that I had actually *rung* her dad to say his daughter *was* my girlfriend and asking if she would visit me. I must have sent the lovelorn poem another time, the first of many.

With Valerie, a while after the nose had healed and when we were genuinely together

Grandma Fergy in the Mid '60s

The only good thing my Grandma Fergy ever did for me was make a warmed milk-bread poultice for my foot after I stepped on a rusty nail at her shack in Niobrara, Nebraska where there was no indoor running water and an outhouse. Uncle Clyde's place was nearby, accessed across various planks and old doors laid as a path, reaching first his front porch where a wolf was chained underneath. When my mother was in hospital having a third sister for me – my father working away in Greenland on the DEW line – Grandma Fergy was summoned to come and take care of the rest of us living then in Norfolk. All I mainly remember is her constant silent stare and the one day I collected money from my paper round and then that night going for a spin in dad's Chrysler parked outside our house, my sister Melanie taking it with her boyfriend, me along for the drive as my collections bought the gasoline. We whirled it around an empty supermarket car park and slid across straight undulating country roads with that Chrysler's amazing cushioning ride. My task on being dropped back home was to find out if the car's theft had been noticed, and it *was* by Grandma's examining gaze, so I went upstairs to my sister's bedroom, turning on her light as the signal for this discovery. They soon dumped the Chrysler elsewhere in town and wiped it clean, no one any later taking things further, and Grandma Fergy's silent stare continuing its pervasive misery. It was obvious she knew who'd taken the car and this the main reason why she had reported it to the police.

That Moment

In having left America, my family and a notional home, aged 16, I've subsequently lived the rest of my life in the United Kingdom. Although occasionally visiting the States, and with parents and sisters living briefly in England and Belgium, we were essentially separated from one another for most of our lives, and continue to be so. When my mother was ill and dying in 2005, I did make two important visits to be with her, albeit briefly when managing to get leave of absence from work. On the second and final visit, when she was bedridden at home, I was overwhelmed with the care being given there by my three sisters and niece. That she had for so long before this been able to live near them is a blessing I have always loved, increasingly so in these years beyond and the feelings I continue to have about my leaving: not regret – it is what I did and how I made a life for myself – but sadness. Mom was dying from lung cancer, had all the treatments that ultimately could not save her, and was now understandably frail and reliant on others for everything. She could talk, yet this was little and rare. But we had a moment together, and I know we did. I sat next to the bed holding her hand and telling mom how much her love and support over all the years separated from one another had meant to me. I think she may have expressed her own regret and sorrow about this, feeling she had let me down – perhaps not then, but in previous letters – and I had to correct this. And I did. I know she listened and heard me and understood. She did say something that also made this clear; some acknowledgement which we both shared. I know this and know at the time I was telling myself how I must not forget this. Ever. Of course, I have – the actual words said, but I knew this would happen so I demanded of myself then that I always remember we had that moment. And we did.

Decision Day

Tedding hay in a field the closest to where I lived, the first time ever I think for that particular job and in that particular field at William Paul & Sons where I got my first full-time occupation as a farm worker: this is where I was on the day I decided to become a teacher: There were many other regular, personal tasks over a year, but this aerating of the hay is what I was undertaking when deciding to teach – the relentless up and down / up and down of driving a tractor on my own had become tedious after nearly three years of whatever lone mechanised field-work had been allocated to me on any given day. When working with others there was the camaraderie, and the social interaction, like teaching Big Ricky how to disco dance. There was that time I was in a convoy of tractors filling trailers with freshly cut grass to take back to bins for silage, the long waits in a queue meaning I managed to read most of Steinbeck during that week sitting in the tractor cab in-between my turns. But these were not the norm. I chose Westminster College in Oxford for studying, and on my first visit I took an 'entrance' examination which was simply writing a long essay I found apt and easy – a descriptive narrative about farming and tractor driving, this somehow fitting into my selected available theme, and it became a poetic pastoral that romanticised agricultural labouring rather than reflect on the deep ennui of repetitiveness which had prompted my decision to be there and so tested on my suitability for a new profession.

At Wherstead Farm – one of the two at Wm Paul & Sons – but not my personal tractor: I used whatever was available

On the Day Hendrix Died

Marooned in Oakland, Iowa, it was a limbo having been in transit back to the UK but turned around at Omaha airport because my father had said it was OK to travel on the family passport I had. Waiting for my individual one to arrive, Hendrix died and I went down to my basement room to cry on the bed, genuinely saddened for his loss but also my still being in America. One day I recorded a spontaneous and lengthy reflection called 'Outside' on a cassette recorder, my first and last narrated poem, observing out of the turret-windows, describing my looking *past* all the things I could see and looking *through* and *beyond*, and then near its end the *half-light* and the *full dark room* as dusk began to fall. When I read now, I hear Carver in its simplicity, so many years before I discovered his genius and was myself regularly prolix as a writer. This was a stopgap town for the family, my dad always on the move through jobs, and one day my mother asked if I would go with the family to church – before I left for England: this small-town requisite for validation from smaller minds and their controls. I refused, as she knew I would – her respecting this – but asking again and explaining the expectations that would help make her staying a fitting-in for however long required, but I would not budge. Sadly gone, if we were together again back then and she asked once more, I would so want to comply, understanding the pressures I was managing to escape and did so forever – and from her – though also knowing I would still not succumb, as she knew for the rest of her life.

Teaching Perspective

The learning curves in teaching are general but also highly personal. Apart from professional skills acquired over time, character and self-confidence matter. My instinct was to be honest if using personal experience as a stimulus for writing or other, obviously applying judgement. Passion was a significant prompt too, as long as this wasn't obsession or dangerous allegiance. This could get complex, so here's an example: as a CND member in the 80s, I was usually careful about not promoting a stance on the obvious 'nuclear bomb' issues in the classroom, but I did once give an impromptu simulation on how to attempt building a shelter from the then UK advice in its *Protect and Survive* pamphlet. Trying by hand to remove the classroom door from its hinges – this a main requisite part of the 'protective' construction – I continued a brisk and histrionically failed attempt to make anything remotely useful (!) from upturned tables propped on a few classroom chairs. I'd delivered this with as much comic energy as I could, and it seemed to have been received well as yet another manic bit of fun from me. This was on a Friday before half term, and on returning to school a week later, I was informed that one of my students had had a despondent break at home, suffering terribly from the emotional turmoil of my demonstration. The mother who'd written to the school about my actions did so with remarkable restraint and, it seems, the intention to educate rather than complain about me, and this was the similar generous corrective delivered by my Deputy Head.

Elk Horn Footwear

When breakfast was over and I was already in my school boots, I would sneak to the stairs and – out of sight – run to the basement bedroom where I could change into Sunday's shoes, the ones that laced up at the side. The footwear I had on was not in the least bit attractive though they were the ones I was expected to attend and be practical in, which they would be if you worked in a factory or on a farm: they were shit-brown coloured with orange-tanned laces and heavy like the weight of two small dead animals. They were not for being chased by girls in the playground, if I was lucky, which could happen by running in my swapped church pair, aged seven or eight and beginning to sense something exciting deep within when caught and touch-tagged. I would feel this as well just walking in those side-lace dress ones, so young and yet confident about how a look defined through expectations. I also had galoshes, which I escaped wearing, growing beyond, as when playing dress-up maybe two years later with my neighbour, suddenly thrilled as she moved around in, I'd guess now, her mother's high heels.

College Literary Society

At my civic college I'd somehow become a committee member of a small student group running a social club in a building we few seemed to occupy with a kitchen, a snooker room, and a Gestetner in an upstairs office used to produce poetry collections in which my and occasional other voices were launched. I later managed to set up a college Literary Society, becoming chairman and given funds for its running and paying for guest speakers. I only clearly recall two of these, the first a resonant one as it was the fine poet Ted Walker, a favourite of mine, and he gave a reading mainly from *The Night Bathers* as well as those soon to appear in *gloves to the hangman*, and afterwards a few of us went on for a meal. I have a firm reminiscence of Ted and his wife being forbearing, gracious listeners to my drunken poetic observations, though we never kept in touch afterwards. The second I won't name, a notorious drinker, and when he stood up in the pub where we were holding his reading – whatever number pint in hand – he fell forward, his beer washing the small audience, and him incapacitated for the night. I was later arrested by the police for 'stealing' a beer mug, my having left the premises to simply finish the drink in it. I had fingerprints taken at the station along with a mug shot, though I was later let off with a caution. The reality was they hadn't found any drugs when I was grabbed for my misdemeanour which had me in the police car's back seat reciting lyrics from *Alice's Restaurant* all about my terrible crime and, of course, 'creatin' a nuisance'.

The 'Committee'

Police Raid

A policeman had entered through the shop into Bob's living room where we were, and he was pointing a gun at us. Bob and I had remained friends after a brief falling-out a few years before, my now regularly spending time at his home in Putney, aged 17-18 years old and continuing to write under his older influences. His flat was behind the shop he ran for his elderly father – Bob no longer a social worker – a traditional corner tobacconists, so as well as cigarettes it stocked newspapers, magazines, confectionary, random grocery items and kids' cheap toys. My friend Sam used to come with me for these stays and this was a time for all kinds of new experiences, mainly listening to albums Bob could afford to buy because he earned, as well as experimenting with a range of poetry writing and other things. Left on our own that night, we'd over-indulged on many things, laughed uncontrollably, watched wallpaper moving for that novice time, and passed out on the floor. On returning home, Bob and his friends couldn't get into the flat because we'd mistakenly bolted a door from inside, and they couldn't wake us after shouting, as well as banging on the doors and a living room window. I can still see the ridiculous fit of the tiny helmet on a hirsute head and absurdity of the plastic pistol pointed at us by one of Bob's more thoughtlessly spaced friends who eventually broke in through the shop – grabbing his play police accoutrements on the way – but this is a deferred discernment when in its moment and you are still tripping.

Oregon Readings

It is a little odd that having left America I ended up giving two poetry readings back there and after I had stopped doing these in the UK. This was much later in life and visiting family, the second reading not that many years ago in Medford at a presentation evening organised for teachers by my sister Julie, a fellow professional. The first was in Ashland in 1997 when a few teaching colleagues and I took students from the UK to stay with Ashland peers and their families. We ran creative activities at the High School, one on Shakespeare, leading to a performance, and mine were poetry workshops, the most successful introducing humuments (erasure) where writers poetically subvert/deface various texts, these books in this case donated from the school's library and which proved popular: to destroy and create. At the performance evening which ended our visit, I read a selection of the students' work and then poetry that would be in my first collection *Nearing the Border* the following year. Some of my family living there attended, including my mother and father, and one of the poems I read was about my dad, his baking sweet cinnamon rolls and other domestic, cooking references. I should have read a poem about my mother, but I'm not sure I had one at the time, directly, and that is a sad irony as I was closest to her, always, and when thinking of this now I imagine her deep hurt, not that she would have shown it. I forget but hope I didn't also read the poem titled *Fishing* – for me, one of the strongest I have ever written – this also about my father when he and his best friend took me fishing as a young boy out high above a raging Niobrara River, our walking across the disused railway bridge and me trying to match their great adult strides when struggling fearfully over the same from behind: having to look downwards to place my steps, I could see the wildness through those huge gaps between ties. We somehow climbed down to sit on one of the concrete stanchions beneath the bridge's great height, and I immediately dropped my bamboo pole into the torrent below, petrified. Although not implied in the poem which focused on a young boy's fear (yet with a gesture of hope at its end), it was at heart about a thoughtless and frightening arrangement, this not new, and there were so many alternative kindnesses and cheer my mother had given me throughout my childhood and beyond which I failed to read about and share with her and all the others on that celebration night.

Farmers Weekly Poetry

Five years of farming have retained a lasting significance in my life, even The Ennui of Tedding: not a poem title (yet) though I will return here to agriculture's impact on my writing. There are many skills learned then that have lived on with me, not least those which are obviously farming-related, but also the DIY skills – agricultural work involving regular building and repair chores – these applied at home as a teacher when for years I certainly couldn't afford to pay for professionals to come in and fix/make things. *Farmers Weekly* magazine played its part in promoting my expertise, the first when I advertised my skills in exchange for free accommodation to attend studies in Oxford, getting two immediate offers and taking up the one on a farm near Stokenchurch and the M40 with a three-bedroom house, requisite weekend work in lieu of rent, and otherwise paid summer holiday agricultural labouring. The second was when the magazine published one of my 'farming' poems. I'd won first prize in *The George Crabbe Memorial Poetry Competition, 1979,* this for a poem titled 'Horse-Witch' about Tom, a retired farm worker living near my cottage in Belstead, my writing about his secretive, magical horseman skills. I therefore had this precedence and obviously referred to it in my submission letter, but it wasn't a poem I included. I was not in fact delighted with the one they did select, though perhaps it isn't surprising they'd deferred on my more experimental concrete and found poems submitted, like the visual representation of cultivating perfect straight lines, or my repeating grid of phrases about potato riddling, bagging these, and in mini-breaks from the conveyor-belt intensity of this job, teaching Big Ricky modern dance moves for our occasional outings to Tracy's nightclub in Ipswich. But I am actually grateful for what was published because national exposure as a poet is much appreciated, especially when just starting out as a writer, and they chose a sonnet – so a poetic convention for a conservative audience – titled 'Showing Cow 979', this recounting my being persuaded/pressganged to lead one of William Paul & Sons' farm heifers inside a ring at the Suffolk County Show in the early '70s. This my first and last time, I led the cow out with a muzzle-rope and wearing a Showman's fleetingly pristine white coat, that Friesian taking off almost immediately, me hanging on, and the predictable result summed up in my sonnet's closing couplet, '…I keep up, holding on, white coat flapping in its / pace, until she breaks free, my trip landing me in pats of bits.'

Wearing a pristine white Show coat with 979 before 'we'
took flight

Grandpa and *The Science of Man*

My grandpa was born in 1885 and I know little of his parents and other origins, but he spent part of his childhood at Elim Children's Home in Elk Horn. A man with little formal education, he later worked on farms in the Atlantic and Council Bluffs Iowa areas, then filed for a homestead in North Dakoda although he did not prove up on his claim, returning to Iowa and worked at a hardware store back in Elk Horn where my mother was born and I lived for a brief period in the early 60s. I do have the happiest memories of being with him and my grandmother, most of these at Christmases, but we as a family moved to Germany in '65 and that is where I was when he died. Sometime after, I acquired his wallet and more recently have used its contents to extrapolate about the person he was beyond a loving, inherently wise man and grandparent. In addition to a driving licence, doctor's diet card and a shopping list, he had two calling cards, one of a *Dr RFG Spier, Associate Professor of Anthropology, University of Missouri,* and at the top my grandpa had written 'The Science of Man'. In searching I did find a reference to the book *Graphic Teaching Aids in Basic Anthropometry,* R. F. G. Spier, D. R. Henning, J. R. Vincent. 'The Science of Man' reference is presumably from the David Hume 18th century text *A Treatise on Human Nature.* The other calling card was of *Aasta May Carlson,* just her name, my mother's, and Danish in origin as was the town of Elk Horn, the Carlson family, and a history/heritage in my childhood days with growing-up intimations but otherwise untainted by the wider darknesses of my later teenage years and reasons for leaving such a mean-spirited example of human nature. Its anthropological study has been inadvertently narrated in many of these anecdotes and asides: a calling card – it would seem – of continuing dismay.

Laissez Faire

Two of the students were late, maybe by 20 to 30 minutes, and everyone else was waiting at the café as agreed, ready to leave. It was annoying but also concerning as we were in an unfamiliar place – Paris! – and they'd all been told not to stray from that area on arrival and given time to explore independently in a minimum of pairs. An RATP bus arrived and the two got off all smiles, but apologising, and when I asked where they'd been, both were so proud to tell me how they decided to see the Eiffel Tower on their own some miles away. I'm not sure which of the nine annual French exchanges this was, though we were only taken twice in that time for a day out to Paris. Each year we linked with a school in Brittany to spend our week, producing a bilingual newspaper at the Foire de Caen as well as the Devon County Show when they returned to us. These were nine years of the richest educational and enjoyable experiences, freedoms in learning you couldn't risk today, not that I was approving of the laissez faire attitude of my two tourist students. It was the first year's exchange on the early morning ferry returning home from Roscoff to Plymouth that I found one student Matt on an upper deck breaking open a 24-bottle case of lagers. Luckily, I'd spotted him and the fact there were few others around, so when I got to him and explained it didn't create a good look for a school trip and me as the teacher in charge, he was most genial in acknowledging the sense of my observation, apologising too, and placing the case of beer carefully back in his large holdall before moving off.

Being a Lutheran

My historical Christianity is owed, for as long as it existed, to convention, expectation and childhood: I have one picture of me aged about seven dressed ready for church and looking like Bart Simpson wearing a suit with bowtie. I do remember the sermons as a visual entity with lunch afterwards. The peak of my religious acquisition was attending classes for Confirmation at the Army chapel in Paul Revere Village – though not being a military family, we lived in the city of Karlsruhe. And because we were in Germany, I was confirmed on the Pentecost in 1967 at Dreifaltigkeitskirche (Trinity Church) in Worms am Rhein near to where Martin Luther presented his critique/proclamation. Other than this, my current atheism is the prevailing adherence, yet I do often feel myself informed by some residual protestant work ethic – however that was assimilated – though I also generally give more credit for this to my farm labouring days. But back to my inception into faith and belief: this must be down to those nightly prayers at bedtime, exactly as we see now in nostalgic '60s' movies or homespun TV shows of the time, where the family would gather on knees at the bedside and recite *Now I Lay Me Down to Sleep*. It is genuinely only in more recent years I worked out the meaning of *Foshadie* which I had aped for so many of those night-times – not obviously informed enough then to extrapolate, even in error, as some Latin expression or similar – as my best childlike approximation to the actual *If I should die…*

The Fall

Before Trevor became such a close friend, I worked with him as the Headmaster who arrived at my school with references from Socrates and the Marguis de Sade. Here was someone who walked a tightrope between the light and dark inside education's complex world. His was the longest and hottest tenure in my time there until he turned into a Phoenix to fly away, yet there were those years of insight and humour before that escape. These were punctuated by several battles between opposing forces: the energies of pragmatism and philosophy; beer-making and motorbikes; poetry and irreverent jokes; cheap suits and belly-tight jeans, or football and local financial management. He delivered sermons on political corruption, massaged a range of egos, used anecdote as a balm for despair, waged war with the local powers that be, and wrote subversive management development plans heavily supported by informed and esoteric quotation. There was always the celebration of teaching and learning. 'Man's yesterday may ne'er be like his morrow. Nought may endure but mutability', and in the relentless educational change from the late 80s through the beginnings of the twenty first century, Shelley's noble maxim was corrupted. Such a sour, intransigent wave on wave affected us all, and some more than others. Trevor tried to hold things together and resist a pace that wasn't tempered with experience or wisdom. His metamorphosis was slow and painful and so he left, but all too soon succumbed to another mythology and ended the struggling lift of his own damaged wings.

Einer der Anderen

I could be an obnoxious 11-12 year old American boy calling out rudely in naive German to girls we passed in the Army school-bus that picked up civilian children to take to Karlsruhe American High School. I was still growing and learning. Paul Revere Village was small-town America inserted along that area of the Rhine with blocks and blocks of military housing and a PX where you could eat fries in its canteen and steal Balfour rings from the department store. At the school site there was an AA Club providing hamburgers for lunch, and at weekends you could go and watch The Mojos play *Gloria* and *Louie Louie*, me singing dirty lyrics to the Kingsmen version. My growing continued there and it's where I had my first fist-fight, a smaller boy talking over *I Had Too Much to Dream Last Night* playing on the juke box, so I pushed him across a table. He challenged me to go outside which is where I was duly beaten up, he taught boxing I'd guess by his Army dad but also good manners as I learned when asked if I'd like to stop – and when I agreed, he shook my hand. To this day I'm not sure if Volksfest and Fasching are one and the same, each merry-making festivity lasting a week or more, but I think the former is what the Germans held at the base where GIs were eager drinkers and a few of us kids were allowed to collect empty bottles to return for and keep their cash refunds; the latter was where the Verkehrspolizei higher up in his crossroads platform was Groucho Marx in black-rimmed glasses with attached eyebrows and moustache, and where walking in the karneval parade I met the gorgeous Ruth Sontag, aged 14 to my then 12, and fell in love.

The Significance of Spelling

It was when living in Norfolk, Nebraska that I learned an indelible lesson about written accuracy. My older sister had a range of Romeo tough guys often calling around for her, competing with one another for macho appeal by burning lit cigarettes in their arms or carving her name along them: being M E L A N I E, it was a significant test of pain and endurance compared with, for example, a J O. I was influenced by them and occasionally had rides in their cool hot rods as a safety-net chaperone for my sister – one time our car-load of hoods being chased by another set as we took escaping fast corners on two wheels. Her entourage was a mix of High School jocks and James Deans, cigarette packets rolled inside T-shirt short sleeves; hair greased back like Ricky Nelson or falling in waves like Sal Mineo. I was 9 going on 10, my girlfriend older at 12, and one night outside her house I used a razor to carve her name in my forearm as she watched. The blade slipped in deep once but I braved things to finish as quickly as I could and went home to clean up the blood. It took some years for the scar to disappear, but for that time I displayed C I N Y as a gradually fading declaration of truncated love – not because she had dumped me soon after the cut – but my having forgotten to carve in the letter D.

Other Culture Wars

On my first day at Chantry Secondary Modern in Ipswich I arrived as smartly dressed as I could be for making a good starting impression. I wore a yellow short-sleeved shirt and a pair of baby-blue slacks, these complemented with yellow socks and a pair of baby-blue sneakers. This was trendy Ivy League in design, but a garish anathema and unwelcome signposting at an English school where everyone wore a uniform, this news to me. I toned things down the following day, wearing a paisley-print shirt, hanging out, and tight but black jeans with Beatle boots. This didn't stop someone singing 'Yankee Doodle Dandy' at me in a corridor and we had a fight soon stopped by a passing teacher. I was the all-American boy with a Beach Boys haircut and having to learn quickly beyond alternative approaches to subject teaching. It didn't take long for so many of my anchors and assumptions to be challenged and altered, direct and indirect questioning of how I behaved becoming a constant war over identity. But it became a permanent change, though I never wore a full uniform, going for a double-breasted blazer and purple tie, and Mr Webber the Headmaster – a great man – once shouting from his flung-open office window *When in Rome Ferguson, do as the Romans do!* which was a warming acknowledgment of my continuing independence within the conforming to a new reality.

Salaam Alaikum

When as a family we arrived in Germany in 1965 to meet up with my father already there, we all lived first in Durlach, a suburb of Karlsruhe, in a small basement flat, my three sisters and me sharing one bedroom. My dad was a civilian but working for the military so we lived on the 'economy', able to use the Army base for schooling and shopping and going for Sunday lunch at the NCO Club and watching movies afterwards in the same large hall, the only one I remember being *Fail Safe*, this after arriving from Elk Horn and the Cuban missile crisis. My sister Melanie made the most of being abroad, getting out and about meeting people, for example the GI who would be her future husband, as well as the Persian guys who were living in Karlsruhe and, like so many other migrant labourers, working manual jobs in a fast-growing economy, not that I understood this then. I was again a chaperone to her, a younger sibling *having* to attend as a kind of personal security, once more my not knowing/understanding this at the time. I have two powerful, positive memories of this acquaintance: once being invited to eat at their shared home, and recall – though so many years ago – it was a beautiful and exotic chicken and rice meal with other entirely unfamiliar accompaniments and our hosts' gracious, kind company. It's hard to explain because this is about influence and feelings, but I will never forget the palpable sense of safety and support being with them. The other was when the men took us – or just me – to an Italian ice cream parlour where I prevaricated over a choice of flavours, saying (I think) how I didn't mind, and being firmly counselled by one of the men on how when asked it was polite to be decisive and rude to be vague. To this day, whenever I offer coffee or tea to a visitor at my home and they respond with a pathetic, 'polite' indecision, I give them that lesson, taking my deliberate and genuinely respectful time to tell them exactly where and how it was learned.

With my sisters – Julie, Melanie, Patty – in Durlach, Germany, 1965

At War with Mr Wood

Mr Wood was my English teacher at Chantry and but for a 'thimble full of petrol' needed to fuel his own running-on-empty vehicle, he'd have managed to catch Rommel and his tank in the North African desert and put an end to the General's role there and then. Mr Wood would occasionally be writing on the board and suddenly stop, clutching his back and groaning – waiting for a concerned ask – or just telling the class about the pain of his old war wound. He always disliked and was mean to me, but I was still placed in his English top set when I'd arrived, no doubt his experiment with my American's aptitude and ability for the subject. A secondary modern, the school aped grammar school modes (as I was to learn) with a House system, the Headmaster wearing a gown, and Mr Wood operating a ranking system for sitting in his class after regular tests and measurements, my moving down the placements and indicative seating gradations quickly. Most of the time was spent copying from the board or completing exercises from Newson's *The Art of English* where I learnt the Figures of Speech and how to précis, some of this formality proving useful in later life but acquired through the dullest of routines. The only liveliness was in random classroom debates, my always willing to express an opinion and have it corrected by Mr Wood, dismissively: perhaps an intention to strengthen my resolve for the future, though I doubt it. I will begrudgingly consider this because he did once agree to provide an interpretation of Jim Morrison's *The Celebration of the Lizard King*, this printed inside the gatefold sleeve of The Doors' *Waiting for the Sun* album I brought in with Mr Wood playing some of the long track on his classroom record player before delivering a summation. As a teacher myself, I do know that elements of the teaching inevitably rubbed off, much of this to do with good friends I made who were in the class, and my own occasional inclinations to learn, or simply absorptions over which I had no control. But so much was thwarted by my own inabilities, lack of sustained effort and the too often withering environment. One task – inherently good, but not under Mr Wood's intense scrutiny – was to learn and recite a poem to the rest of the class, my choice (or given) being John Donne's 'Death Be Not Proud'. To this day I can still recite, but only up to the point where I failed and stopped back then in 1968/9: *Death, be not proud, though some have called thee / Mighty and dreadful, for thou art not so; / For those whom thou think'st thou dost overthrow / Die not, poor Death, nor yet canst thou kill me*, and to employ a clichéd rhetorical strategy that Mr Wood no doubt taught me back then, I'll pick up on the allusion to say how he didn't kill my spirit or desire for independent thinking and progression and, above all, resolve to make personal progress. It might have been interesting for him to hear from me that I became an English teacher too, but I would doubt a genuine connection – Mr Wood I'd imagine stopped short again in a different desert of engagement.

Driving with Uncle Glenn

Travelling between Elk Horn and Omaha on the I-80 with Uncle Glenn was a major achievement of my childhood in that I did the driving, sitting on his lap, hands on the steering wheel, occasionally honking at the cars I was overtaking. Aged 5-8, I never had prior formal training and was obviously a natural. He was always a father-figure, and my middle name is Glenn which was a wise decision made by his youngest sibling Aasta. When I stayed at Uncle Glenn's in Council Bluffs, I'd sleep in his huge basement room, sometimes sitting like an adult at the huge desk down there and looking at some of his moderately adult magazines. An insurance adjuster, going on daytime journeys with him to collect premiums or similar meant less of me driving – these would be unfamiliar roads – but more in the joy of having stacks of pancakes with an excess of maple syrup for roadtrip breakfast in truckers' cafes. Uncle Glenn was a complete comfort zone. I don't remember ever being scolded or corrected or denied; I also do not remember ever being over-indulged.

With Uncle Glenn, Omaha, March 1959

Karlsruhe American High School

Two teachers at this high school made a positive, lasting impression on my life. The first was my English teacher Mr Voeller who wrote 'May you continue to follow the newest in fashions and suaveness' in the *Autographs* section of my *Der Kavalier* '67 Yearbook, and though I had to look up the last word, it was one of a number of kindnesses he conveyed in such simple ways to boost a young boy's ego. I know the comment was prompted by my once wearing purple corduroy flares and a garish yellow silk shirt on a 'free-dress' school day, so the observation was perhaps as much about my daring extravagance as elegant choice. The other was my German teacher Gertraud Schlegel. Though I spent a significant proportion of our lesson time together standing outside her classroom for too much talking – and I don't mean speaking in German which I never quite acquired – she had still seen something of promise in my attitude, perhaps here its independent streak. For her signing of my Yearbook (you always sought out favourite teachers for this) she had written *Welche Regierung die beste sei? Diejenige, die uns lehrt, uns selbst zu regieren*, though luckily she penned it in English: *What is the best government? That which teaches us to govern ourselves*, by 'Wolfgang von Goethe', and I know this wasn't a remedial to behaviour but a trust in my ability to learn lessons later in life.

47

Lawrence's Assembly

It was in the early years of my teaching when John, the Deputy Head, was reading a poem by Lawrence with the repeated word 'ugliness, ugliness'. The message was ironically apt and I considered it as a waft of ever more stale air circulating above the heads of most of the students in the school hall. All I could think about was an article I'd once read on D.H. titled *Lawrentian Stillness,* all about sexual parameters and similar Freudian allusions. I knew the students thought they were all being shafted standing there in that baking assembly on a hot summer's day. It smelt like a gym changing room. I was waiting for a hymn about sweat and then a prayer for spiritual deodorant, but apart from the fact we didn't have 'religious' assemblies anymore, it would have taken a first-time collective chorus to raise any olfactory miracles that day. The students were made to stand because the whole school had to be packed into a hall built for just over half of them. Then one boy fell: straight forward like one of those military guards on a sweltering parade. He didn't bend, just dropped flat on his face having bifurcated a couple of giggling peers in front of him. Almost immediately, two other students carried him out like a broken door. John didn't bat an eyelid and finished the poem. I don't think the public at large then or even now fully appreciate just how professional teachers sometimes have to be.

Finding a Father for $9.95 and Other Numbers

For 5 cents short of 10 dollars, all I actually bought were numbers in the online *Omaha World-Herald* archive, allowed 30 downloads in 24 hours and yet little of any new revelations in the digital newspaper records about my personal history: the unknown father, and a brother or sister too – my blood-sibling still with us, possibly – 2 years younger than me, but there were no mentions in *Births* for that May in '56 and this person I was trying to find, if still alive, nor of me, surprisingly, in an otherwise documented March of '54. Over 60 years ago and none the wiser. But my other sister was announced in 1960 with our new dad, 6 years further along in time, yet in a different Omaha road. I found the pictures of a childhood home, number 1406 on North 40th, the duplex's concrete porch still staring out at the passing cars as the years rolled by: thousands and thousands, some still in primer grey waiting for their changes. My father Olin, a school automotive mechanics teacher, was mentioned 13 different times in termly staffing confirmations over the years, but there was only 1 quote of '*his* boys work hard' – students with him in 1961, Oct 29.

Before and after ... Boys do complete job.

New Paint Room Gives Tech Full Auto Body Shop

Tech High School's new paint room offers boys wishing to learn the auto body-and-fender trade an opportunity to do the complete job.

The paint room was completed for use this semester. A brick wall was laid by Tech masonry students and when the Board of Education added paint and ventilation facilities the total cost came to seven thousand dollars.

Olin Stanfield, Tech students' instructor in auto mechanics, said his boys work hard at becoming craftsmen.

Two, Gordon Nordstrom, 1801 North Thirty-fourth Street, a senior, and Dale Wininger, 4720 North Thirty-sixth Avenue, a junior, were photographed working on a Board of Education truck, getting the vehicle ready for painting. Both boys said they are interested in obtaining jobs in auto body work after graduation.

The cars taken into the new paint room are sprayed by the boys after all dents, scratches and rust spots have been removed. After the painting the car is left to dry in the room and the ventilation system insures absence of dust particles settling on wet paint.

The students have painted about eight cars this semester.

Sunday World Herald, Omaha, Oct 29, 1961,
'Youth Activities'

50

Where Were You on the 9th August, 1974?

I was at Kesgrave, Ipswich, watching Richard Nixon's 3am (UK time) resignation speech on the TV, and it was just a short while after he was finished and I had written my newspaper article for the local *Evening Star* that I was riding my Honda C50 into town delivering its critical summary, with comments, to their offices. Technically, his speech was given on the 8th – just in case any historians are already asking questions – but it was as obnoxious in any time zone. It can be hard to convey the impact of his insufferable lies and excuses when placed in the context of current political obfuscations or, more accurately, the universal norm of blatant evasions and denials, or even just total ignoring, but I was most outraged by Nixon's appropriation of words from Theodore Roosevelt, as if another's principled articulation could transmute to ennoble and frame his actions. This is what he said in concluding: *Sometimes I have succeeded and sometimes I have failed, but always I have taken heart from what Theodore Roosevelt once said about the man in the arena, "whose face is marred by dust and sweat and blood, who strives valiantly, who errs and comes short again and again because there is not effort without error and shortcoming, but who does actually strive to do the deed, who knows the great enthusiasms, the great devotions, who spends himself in a worthy cause, who at the best knows in the end the triumphs of high achievements and who at the worst, if he fails, at least fails while daring greatly."* By the time I got back to Kesgrave where I stayed the night at my girlfriend's house rather than my Belstead cottage – she possessed a television and I didn't – I had to almost immediately leave again as my work on the farm back near home began at 7am, my not yet a writer of any meaningful description, and certainly not a journalist, though had I accepted the offer of a job a year later at *Concrete Magazine* (building/construction) when I went to their London offices for interview, I might well have been.

Lunging Ring

Having cromed/cultivated my perfect straight lines after a field had been ploughed, what I despised was later seeing one of the sons from that William Paul farm riding his horse across my disciplined pattern of a work ethic. He was no horseman – unlike Arthur who had worked these same acres years before with a jobbing horse and a dried fresher's backbone in his trouser pocket – but just a joyrider. Still, my farm mate Bob and I built him his lunging ring for the weekend cash-in-hand, a faultless round and more with flawless lines of uprights and rails measured exactly by the eye. These were woodmen's skills: felling trees, shaping posts, fencing, making corners strong with an axe to carve out grooves and insert an angled branch to buttress and anchor. Farmhand roots; moving in different circles.

Apostrophe Stinker

Where's Weeley? could have been the chant – I was one of the many few / few many who went to Weeley Festival at Clacton-on-Sea for the weekend of August 27th-29th, 1971. It is estimated up to 150,000 attended and yet this isn't one of the highlights remembered, it seems, in the pantheon of great musical gatherings (obviously not a Woodstock, nor an Isle of Wight) though the line-up was stellar. As ever then in going to similar, a few friends and I went just with blankets and plastic sheeting for ground and cover if needed, no food – and I don't actually recall ever eating there, seriously – the only sustenance a four pint plastic container of Ted's cider from The Black Horse in Ipswich. Drugs could be reliably obtained on site, or at least that was the safe luck of my experience. The music played non-stop throughout the weekend to get through the significant number of seriously famous acts, so if you slept you missed whatever was on at that time. Some of those big names playing were the Faces, Rory Gallagher, Quintessence, Mott the Hopple, Colosseum, Edgar Broughton Band, Juicy Lucy, Arthur Brown, Mungo Jerry, Barclay James Harvest *with* a Symphony Orchestra (40 piece), Lindisfarne, King Crimson, T-Rex and Van der Graff Generator. There were more, and I managed to tape many on a battery-operated cassette recorder. I even captured an extraordinary moment of emotive coincidence with King Crimson performing *Cirkus* while someone in the crowd was having, we guessed, a bad trip. As the music lulled then built slowly back to a crescendo, those around the struggling person were shouting for a doctor – from desperate individual pleas to an occasional chorus of yells – with the gantry spotlights finding and illuminating the cluster to direct helpers there just as the music reached a dramatic and empathetic peak. There was also the infamous

Where's Wally? chant, a fight between caterers and the Hells Angels, and a significant field fire, but the most memorable non-musical feature of the event was its toilets, the *Chick's Bogs* and the *Guy's Bog,* misplaced apostrophes the least of the problems, with 'chicks' provided the relative superiority of buckets, while 'guys' had an excavated trench with scaffolding and boards placed above for those needing to sit, this not a misspelling.

My Blood Sibling Bobbie Ann had a Way of Saying Things

Bobbie Ann said our father worked Omaha as a Murray Dance Instructor and that's how he made extra money. He was a terrific swing dancer but not the jitterbug, and he was fair-minded but not a liberal. Bobbie Ann said our father bought older cars, talking to them, and wanted to live to be an Old Fanatic: he had worked at an Oldsmobile dealership – though that's all she knows about this – before teaching school mechanics, and West Coast Swing at other places. Bobbie Ann said our father was never called Olin, but instead Stan, or Swede, and she said back in the day, before birth control, that men, especially some, would spread their 'seed' all over the place and she was afraid Stan was one of those men. Bobbie Ann said unplanned pregnancies were an unfortunate by-product in their eyes and every man would handle this in different ways. Stan was a Leo and so was President Bill Clinton and did I see any connection? Bobbie Ann said he had a sugar way to make a living, a junkie for motorcycles and sweetness – not the Hells Angels – but fixing them up, and finally there was the pain. Bobbie Ann said she remembered him strong all his life, showing off dancing on the motorbikes, the *manly* man, and he was proud of it but wouldn't see the Dr Man. Bobbie Ann said he ate candy and chain-smoked all day long, was proud of it but unable to go back: it was the sugar but he didn't suffer or linger.

Ars Longa Vita Brevis

The Nice album of this vignette's title presented a psychedelia which was a perfect mirror of the genre at its time in 1968: childlike, playful songs mixed with progressive interpretations of symphonic scores. Indeed, that partiality for such bands to pilfer from the Classical catalogue was the catalyst for me and many others my age to take a serious interest in this music at a time when we had little reason to do so otherwise, and I certainly had no nurturing from family for this. The Latin maxim of the album's title and its side 2 suite formed the basis for my English 'O' Level creative writing exam in 1969. Who knows how I was able to use this and its named movements – *Awakening, Realisation, Acceptance, Denial* – but I did, relishing the conscious manipulation to sound knowledgeable and informed. I do vaguely remember enjoying what I wrote and how I incorporated the gist of its aphoristic title in some youthful declaration of creative intent. Pretentious? Absolutely. And of course I did well, but as an eventual English teacher I never lost sight of the fortuity of the terminal examination process this had presented me and thus its many flaws.

Change in LA

Most of the summer of '72 was spent in a bedroom at my parents' suburban home on the outskirts of Los Angeles writing late-teenager *I miss you* love letters for sending back to England. I also played the guitar and listened to music – mainly the Amboy Dukes. Or I'd be in the living room on a recliner watching football, smoking Salem menthols and drinking cold beers. One day in intense June heat I tried to dig garden borders around the outside of the concrete-hard, browning back yard lawn. Greener at the front with its underground, automatic sprinkler system, tomato plants grew because the soil had been laid with traces of human effluent and undigested seeds. I'd arrived via my sister's home in Oregon – brother-in-law Bill driving all eleven hours on speed, and after a short sleep he drove back the same, if on a new wave of pills. I made some of that journey down Interstate 5 sitting on an armchair in the back of his yellow pick-up wearing a US navy sailor's hat. Nothing much other than this happened, though I'd gladly go back and hold on to my mom's hand more often than I will have done. One evening Bill's friend Tony came around and took me out for a ride on his motorbike, our long hair streaming in the hot night air, cruising across a large bridge and eventually out of the city to a field where he left me to go further off alone and inspect his marijuana plants, warning me just before moving ahead to beware of the rattle snakes. I stood rigid for whatever lengthy and frightening time he was gone and don't remember anything about getting back home later. The Amboy Dukes' album was 1970's *Marriage on the Rocks/Rock Bottom,* and because of the psychedelic and similar lyrics it was obviously before Ted Nugent became or let the world know he was a dumb redneck.

Ah Sunflowers

We had a teaching supply replacement at Chantry – maternity cover for our regular English teacher – who introduced my 4th or 5th year class to The Fugs, using a study of poetry as an excuse to play their musical version of Blake's *Ah, Sunflower, Weary of Time* taken from their literally named *First Album*. He must have shown pictures as well and I was hooked immediately with the obvious appeal of hippies and poetry and music and, though not with this track, irreverence and rebellion. He also told us they were originally called The Village Fuck – which I don't believe is true – and though a gratuitous appeal to easily titillated youth, it worked. This lanky, informal, eccentric, seemingly worldly-wise and charismatic teacher had a colossal impact on me at the time and opened up new and exciting horizons, musical and poetic, for which I will always be grateful. As an English teacher I've also played The Fugs to my students, continuing the subversive line, my choice from their later album *It Crawled into My Hand, Honest*. It was *Johnny Pissoff Meets the Red Angel* from Side 2 of the album which begins with the redneck tirade of Johnny – his racist and homophobic rant as manic and real as it was then and still is today: a potentially dangerous parody because of this realism, which I warned students about then, but won't actually repeat its words here, things having quite likely worsened, incredibly. But the diatribe isn't left unanswered. In another musically beautiful twist, Johnny's angry persona is answered by the graceful Country Rock harmonies of the Red Angel who seeks to change Johnny's ways with its wisdom and urgings for peace: *Ahimsa, oh Johnny, ahimsa! / In the spinning confusion, ahimsa! / In the blood of life, death, and torture, / Ahimsa! Ahimsa! Ahimsa! / Ahimsa, is the seashell of Buddha. / Ahimsa, is the rose and the lamb –* (Ahimsa is a

Sanskrit term meaning 'peace' and translates as 'no violence', or 'no himsa'). I didn't play their Gregorian chant based on synonyms for *Marijuana*, its title, which as satire and protest is musically beautiful – sensibly never entering the drugs anecdotes arena, and certainly never endorsing by any mentioning whatsoever, and whatever my own positive experiences. I may have played one or two other oddments from the array of comic snippets that make up most of the rest of that album's side, like the ditty *Life Is Funny*, sung in the most morose of tones: *life is funny, life is free, got all of them goodies coming to me, it's so funny I could cry, it's so funny you could die, it's so funny…*, and I felt then as I do now that the elliptical existentialism of that ending is...

The Importance of Music in 1971: 1

If only allowed one album out of all that I have and even all that are available from forever, it would be John Martyn's *Bless the Weather*. And if, similarly, I was only allowed one song out of all those available in the infinite musical universe, it would be *Head and Heart* from the album. This third solo LP presents John at his sweetest – the sweetest songwriting, the sweetest vocal and the sweetest guitar playing, all as on opener *Go Easy* with its honeyed guitar chords and the youthful vocal register so different to the gruff slur and growl of John's eventual vocal instrument. Second *Bless the Weather* is a classic in the broadest sense, but also in Martyn's oeuvre: the distinctive slap-guitar playing of John himself and then the accompaniment of great pal and genius, double bass player Danny Thompson – a match made in whatever sonic heaven oversees such musical gifts bestowed on this aural world. It is where John subsequently roared and joked in a Glaswegian accent utterly incomprehensible and yet innately and cosmically endearing. The expressions of emotion in both these opening tracks reflect all of the happy hope and positive romanticism for life and love I then had a right to wish for and now embrace wherever it was achieved and still endures – whatever loss being tempered by the beautiful expression of that initial idealism. And then there is sixth *Head and Heart*, a song gently but profoundly honest in its expression of love and where fear is so much a part of its declaration. The guitar work is once again definitive Martyn with the slap and pluck of the rhythm and then quick lead licks, Thompson bending his notes and running them up and down in that magical musical partnership and along with the lyrical poetry of its lines. The penultimate instrumental *Glistening Glyndebourne* introduces a jazz aura that would become an increasingly strong influence in

Martyn's writing and performance; but more importantly, it introduces the electro-acoustic cosmos of Martyn's guitar world, here presented through the Echoplex prism which electronically echoed and repeated and swirled the beautiful melodies and skills of John's playing. It was at Essex University in Colchester – just up the A12 from Ipswich – where I first heard John playing with his Echoplex. Having gone to see and hear this acoustic folk god that *Bless the Weather* had introduced, he at some stage in the set and without warning flicked a switch somewhere on a machine and in my as well as most other unsuspecting heads, and this psychedelic tsunami of echoing sound surged through the PA which, as they say, blew me away.

When I Wasn't Gary Oldman

Unable to speak French, I couldn't explain I wasn't Gary Oldman. I'd been here before, not that Derrida mistook me for an actor, this situation occurring fourteen years later and ironically my now running the school's French exchange: still quite incapable of doing more than order a coffee, say hello/goodbye, and – at my most expansive – announcing 'en avant' when in charge of both the English and French students. The girl had been staring at me for ages, not continuously, but looking up from her meal and across that tent-restaurant with a classic long hard cold gaze to where I was also eating. We were both sitting at our respective tables with other people, me with French colleagues as we worked on our bilingual newspaper *Images* at the Foire Internationale de Caen. It was lunchtime in a packed dining area there, and the staring had become unnerving as well as annoying. When she got her friends to turn and look too, saying something about me, I was also getting angry. Eventually walking over, there was understandable tension, and as the girl spoke directly to me, I gave the international sign of being ignorant in foreign languages by shrugging shoulders and looking stupid. What she then explained to my French friends was that the film *Léon: The Professional* was currently showing in town and she wondered if I was the famous actor Gary Oldman starring in this. I'll never understand how she conjured the extrapolation I'd be physically in Caen because of also appearing on the big screen there, though I was more than happy at that moment, and to this day, to be so adamantly mistaken for a fine actor with notably distinguished bonnes allures.

Maxine and Emery

I was sure Aunt Maxine had hit me over the head with a broom for misbehaving, though I had no idea why, apart from the fact it wasn't her and instead a blue jay which swooped down to swipe me with her wing – as I was later told and because I'd been taking an interest in her fledglings stranded on the ground. Maxine and Uncle Emery lived in Elk Horn, Emery the second eldest Carlson sibling who, apart from serving in the South Pacific in WWII when he was wounded, stayed his whole life in the town, becoming the Postmaster there. I have the happiest memories of their home and their hospitality, this above and beyond in looking after Mom and her children when we were in transit and in limbo and in difficulty. It was a generous welcome. I especially recall chasing fireflies at night in their back garden as well as laying hessian sacks out over the watered lawn to catch nightcrawlers, using our flashlights to spot when lifting the bags and then pulling them out by hand. I think we sold our collections or gave away as bait for fishing. Cars always feature in my reminiscences of being/living in Elk Horn: Grandpa's big dark Oldsmobile or Buick – not that I really know – with its chewing-tobacco-infused smells and his slow, secure drives into town; my steering of Uncle Glenn's with his hands under mine *just* for a place to rest them, and Emery backing out of his drive in whatever large automobile he had then, spinning his steering wheel around with its Brodie knob that was so coolly smooth in its appearance and the car's graceful turn.

Lorraine's Letter

Having found my father Olin's Papillion, Nebraska home address online in 2009, I did eventually send a letter introducing myself and asking the obvious questions. Lorraine replied, apologising for the lateness, writing about the brutal winters and therefore spending these in Texas with her 'boyfriend' which let me know before she explained that Olin had passed, and it was in 1989. I couldn't be surprised, or even saddened, because of never knowing him, and all of the years, but there was disappointment in the immediate end of the story, or so I thought. Lorraine told me she had been *his third wife or maybe 4th!! Who knows!* and then began to detail all I needed to learn. When they met he'd already had two kids, Bobbie Ann (who I eventually met in Vegas), and Scott who'd died a few years before her letter. Olin had come to Omaha in '54 with *a car racing group*, getting work in a garage and later a job in the public school system – Tech High – as a *shop/mechanic instructor*. He had a pilot's licence, was a radio ham, and for a big man – *not tall, but broad shoulders and big boned* – he was *a beautiful dancer*. As a school instructor *he was tough and the boys respected him* so all of this meant he was little like me and I certainly wasn't like him. Even in the photographs she sent I couldn't see a resemblance, though later Bobbie Ann always insisted there was. It also struck me that in 1989 I was still relatively early into my teaching career, had struggled to just get a mortgage on a house and was raising a young family, and if I'd had the will as well as the internet then, I wouldn't have tried to track him down.

Cross-Country

My school's cross-country course was genuinely rural. The woods where it really started were a few hundred metres down the road from the sports hall. I'd watched hawks or some type of bird of prey scouting from tree to tree when I'd run through. One part was a public footpath cutting across a large farmer's field and in the winter the mud would suck shoes off your feet. Whilst it wasn't particularly hilly, there was a long slow climb back towards the school near the end. Then it was two laps on the school field. I liked to run. Whenever we could, Kev and I would go out at lunch times – when they were longer than they later became, and we were fitter. We would often run the course with the students, but mostly liked to go out on our own. One day it was just the two of us, no different to most running days: the weather basically fine because I wouldn't go out if it was raining. I didn't mind the cold – in fact, the colder the better – but I would not put up with rain. We took the same route and talked the same crap as usual. However, that day we stopped at the plaque in the middle of the woods. Normally, we'd simply pass by because after a while you have to accept that things have happened for a reason. But that day we stopped and had a good long look at the plaque which commemorated the students who got lost, even though they were chaperoned, and never returned having gone out one Friday afternoon to run just for the fun of it.

Karma Reflux

I hope there isn't ever a personalised, self-Karma in older age, retributions for all the free passes and saves dealt in youth by the indulging, tolerant gods. Up for consideration would be that time walking on the outer ledge of Putney Bridge across the Thames. Then there were the races in Pete's Mini Cooper along late-night country lanes, mine and the Stylistics' *Betcha by Golly Wow* inanities spurring him on at speed; or as Lawrence's regular pillion rider urging for explosive take-offs at traffic lights on his Yamaha – both my drivers' sober accelerations operating under the inebriations of my daredevil will. The let-offs in older age seem less acceptable even when this acknowledgement comes from my thankfulness as that continuing survivor – such dumb risks taken when there were by now others to think about. Perhaps the reckonings have already happened and weren't to me personally, and that's a despairing thought: it wouldn't be difficult to locate the payback if looking beyond myself. All those years of being outspoken in a detestation of Job's narrative, the withering control and diminution structured around fear and a promise. I'd never thought of these revenges until now, already made, and perhaps more to come – no weighing out of a balance; the disproportionate, eventually administered, having been worth their long teasing wait by those who actioned them.

Grandpa's Other Two Calling Cards

What we find in a person's wallet can tell or remind us – or prompt guesswork by the same receptions: imagine the gulf between contents of a 60's billfold and 21st century social media threads. Grandpa's driving licence reminded only of car trips into town along that single road from the rise going out of Elk Horn where he lived, down into what became main street to park in that *butterfly* splay, as I'll call it, common in American small towns: the cars at diagonal angles lining the single thruway like splayed wings to each side of the body of it. This licence had the first of two capitalised imperatives, and it was: 'RESTRCTED' to this *town* parameters, but it had always been such a safe ride. His diet sheet startled me – grandpa was a big man but not obese, and he'd worked hard all his life and had wholesome home-cooked food throughout that time (no ready meals or take-aways) so I was surprised, probably naively, that back in 1961 there was already a concern for diet and healthy eating. And then there is the foreboding tone of the opening double negative in the second prohibition, this time including italics: 'DO *NOT* EAT EVEN SMALL AMOUNTS OF *ANY* FOOD NOT ON THIS LIST', a hammering home, though this didn't prevent the diabetes and what he hadn't told anyone about his leg, and the operation that failed.

3 Ton Move

Moving myself and family to Devon for a first teaching job in a hired 3 ton was more than simply being able to on a full UK driving licence: I'd become adept with one, driving for the Co-op in Oxford and delivering furniture. After two years of farm work, I had to move into the city as a consequence of changed personal circumstances that would control things forever. Living in a flat just off the Iffley Road, I still needed to work, not being eligible as an American for a student grant. I did odd jobs here and there, like being a Christmas postie, and another was undertaking industrial cleaning high up in the roofs of the hanger-like car assembly buildings at a Cowley plant. In the summer after my third year and having attained my teaching qualification, I was employed through the holiday, driving and delivering and earning. I didn't work at a paid job in my final fourth year, this being demanding enough, with just studying *The Novel* requiring reading an author's work in a week – perhaps two for Dickens – and having our first daughter also in '79, three days after Christmas. Although the move there had been forced upon us, this was a perfect development, and I considered myself lucky to be at home when other dads would have to go to their jobs, this giving me so much time with Ana from the day of her birth. And late one night, exploring the theory of phrenology and divination with her, I wouldn't then in my new father's reverie have thought how I'd never again believe it possible to predict or even anticipate a personal future.

Counselling Shaun and Ian

Teaching was a forever learning curve, not so much in the subject-specific sense, but in adopting other tangential skills to convey learning beyond what could/would be considered the pedagogical focus – especially that perceived as such by the charlatans. Students Shaun and Ian were not friends, but were similar. They never sat together in lessons and yet shared exactly the same outlook on their educational prospects. Shaun never spoke in class, but Ian was a main contributor – and this was one major difference – yet they both worked hard on assignments and were usually the first to complete tasks set. Shaun was taller than Ian, another difference, but they were both sixteen. Shaun said his bit more often than Ian, which was *I'm stupid, Sir*, but Ian put it his own way often enough, *I'm not as bright as the others*. They both solicited affirmation from me. With Shaun it was *I'm just stupid, aren't I, Sir?* and he tended to always follow this narrow line of enquiry. Ian could be more thoughtful in his anxiety, *I'm not going to get such good grades as the others, will I, Sir?* I was their therapist. Neither wanted me to deny their concerns, but they did seek solace in the soothing words I had to offer. I informed Shaun that he actually worked harder in class than most students. He feigned misery all of the time, but loved it when I reminded him of the joy he derived from this. I informed Ian that he contributed orally better than more academic students – it's the writing that was a problem. We recollected how I no longer had to send him out of the class for behaving like an ass. Shaun could attempt subtlety. *There's not much point in me continuing, is there, Sir?* he'd prompt and we'd then spend five minutes talking about the value of the work ethic. I told him that if I were an employer I'd value his hard graft and effort and then watch him fight back a smile. When the bright girls who sat right in front of my desk teased him and called him handsome, he didn't smile as much as when I told him that he could work for me if I was in the market for a good employee. Ian was more direct and earnest. *What's the point in studying if I never get a pass grade?* he cried at me with big dry eyes. But he too could smile when I told him how he wiped the floor with the brighter but lazy students in the class who were afraid to explore ideas freely and openly. We laughed at how he struggled with his words when reading aloud and yet persevered. I explained what kind of strength that was. Shaun wanted to be a postman. I told him that I'd love to be a postman: here was honest work and it kept you fit. I counselled him that you couldn't play at being glum if you were a postman and his misery turned to genuine concern. But Shaun broke a smile again just for the practice and the girls teased him about how handsome he'd be as a postman and he could deliver love letters to them any time. Ian wanted to join the police, but he'd need to be taller and he'd need to get his pass grade. He loved and admired his father and his father wanted Ian to be a policeman and to get his pass grade. I wanted him to get his pass grade but knew that this would not happen. I counselled Ian that he would continue to learn, as I had done, and that he could always carry on with his education. I quoted Shelley, but not out loud.

Finding France, If Not the Language

Running my school's French exchange was a social and geographical success: taking students and then family there introduced me to people and places in a lasting monolingual love-affair. I'd visited Paris on the educational exchange, journeying up the River Seine with pupils, but I got to the top of the Eiffel Tower with my girls – our trip to the Hard Rock Café another kind of pilgrimage where Conway Twitty's white suit make-believed behind showcase glass. And I wasn't after cheesburgers: when the Calvados was poured on that crêpe and torched until its edges charred, alcohol transcended flame to burn in my throat at a Honfleur restaurant where I wanted to eat outside as a busker sang Marvin Gaye. On Omaha Beach, sand was driven by wind and rain with its shoreline deserted and the otherwise quietness undisturbed. A cold chill pushed me towards that large engraved memorial stone to remind of my other home like a double chord played in the head, as if this should somehow harmonise and remind of those both living and dead. It was the very first school exchange which introduced me to Caen and Normandy and the significance of the Second World War to those living there then, and now. Visiting as part of *The 10 Cities* project organised by Devon Curriculum Advice and supported by a Euro budget, we took a small group of students for the educational experience and to make a film – all those to be made in each city/country involved in the project would be beamed to EU member states via the Olympus satellite. The Mémorial de Caen was a first introduction for me as well as our students to a profound meaningfulness of the horrors that took place there, and of course beyond – its flat expanse of concrete fronting the building like a Normandy plain where ghosts coloured the huge rectangle a faded white headstone. This was reinforced when we went to Pegasus (Bénouville)

Bridge, hoping to film in the area: the site of the first combat of the D-Day Invasion. It was there at the Café where we met its proprietor Arlette Gondrée – aged five at the time of the fight to secure that bridge – and asked if we could film in the surrounds. She informed us that no one was ever allowed to do this in her café, but learning a little about who we were and of our project she said she'd make an exception and we filmed a short segment inside, talking briefly with her. This is where the students and I learned of the deep sense of thankfulness there is for the liberation of the bridge, 'Madame' conveying such with a palpable passion for my British students. I have never forgotten this moment, her sentiment asserting its message of empathy and belonging whenever I have subsequently heard warring charlatans intoning 'sovereignty' in their little-England narratives about Brexit, before and after.

A Woodstock Afternoon

I marked essays in front of the original as Ana was beyond
my closed door and in the other room watching *Woodstock
'94*: dad and daughter spanning these areas and the years
like twins. I didn't need to explain why, for her, there was
no Hendrix with an anthem tossed to violent winds and a
hope for resolution of its once comfortable hymn. She was
doing her English homework as I assessed students'
responses to a difficult play. If we tried, we could have
analysed what it was that made each film a bridge as well
as a growing divide: I could have imagined what was
missed when Sebastian's tie-dye voice had been scraped
across the years to croak and hiss in the version she heard,
but this would only have been my interpretation, and with
it would go the weight of memory and restless expectation.
Her songs would not sing refrains on war, but instead, show
how being rich or poor was the battleground. There'd
always be music to recollect that first contact of touch and
knowing eyes – an electric charge sparked off the initial
note and across time. Sharing this, we were as close and far
apart inside whatever such a mystery intensified. I went into
her room where together we watched a sea of hands convey
bodies in an act of trust. I saw a symbol of a derivative
peace and love and knew she was moving to the side Larkin
saw before this show, but whether I taught her the allusion
as I would to those at school – or ignored its brooding tone
– she would continue to grow to where my love could not
follow but always go.

Record Collection

I'm someone who is, I am sure, within the normal parameters of being anal about their record collection – it is, *obviously*, alphabetised, and *why* would anyone ask if it was? Tom Waits, speaking of his wife Kathleen Brennan's, recalls: *Her record collection and her library were both impressive compared to mine. When I met her most of my records were kind of stuck together with cheese and hair and oil and stuff. She had hers not only still in the cases but still in the little paper sleeves too. That in itself was something of a revelation.* I like the incredulity that the records were still in the paper sleeves. My albums have travelled with me over time and been displayed on a variety of shelving: starting simple in an empty space, being 'contemporary rough' using breeze blocks and planks, moved on to store-bought cheap pine structures, and now the requisite IKEA *Billy* (actually, flashier *Kallax*) units. I once had to move them all upstairs so a room could be decorated, and it cracked the living room ceiling beneath them. Although a core of the albums is from their actual time and my regular listening then, many are from charity shops and occasional online purchases over the years. I also collect new vinyl releases. However, the second-hand market is now popular and prices for originals are beyond that sense of victory when you came across them on the cheap, especially some deceased person's collection donated by the encumbered recipient before they realised its significant value.

Writing for *The Observer*

Between my careers in farming and then teaching, I made a serious attempt at becoming a journalist, writing job application letters to local newspapers or offering my good intentions to various magazine publishers further afield. The most intensive attempt at securing a start was getting my long hair cut specifically for a job interview in Bury St Edmunds that I didn't get. I'd previously refused to have a trim for another interview, acknowledging there I'd need to wear a hair-net for the potential job installing car air conditioning I also didn't get. My next-door neighbour in Belstead was a senior executive with William Paul & Sons, a wonderful man who was genuinely supportive of my youthful hopes, dreams and needs, writing a letter of recommendation for me to a friend of a friend, that first friend writing to his with the opening paragraph 'You will recall at the Chicken Convention at the Hilton we met a charming young man with Mr. A H-M who was named Michael Ferguson and we both said we would help the young man out.' Nothing came of it, and I had never attended that poultry party. The nearest I got to working in journalism was for the then *Concrete Magazine* based in London. This was a journal for the building industry, and at my interview I was warned I'd be starting at the proverbial bottom if offered a position and therefore making loads of tea for others. I can't be sure, but have a suspicion they'd sensed my loftier literary ambitions and were giving me a warning dose of reality, and if I was offered a post – I think so, but am not completely sure – I obviously declined. My first newspaper article was therefore actually published in *The Times Educational Supplement* in 1984 when I was a teacher. It was titled *The Gnomes of Oracy*, a 'Talkback' piece on speaking and listening in the classroom, having developed some expertise on the subject by my fourth year of teaching. I did have a further piece in the *TES*, this seventeen years later and soon after the 9/11 attacks in New York. I had written another comment piece about a class discussion with my GCSE English group of the time and how their need to express thoughts and feelings on that terrible September event had moved and impressed me with its fresh honesty and insight, being a positive catharsis for us all. My *Observer Magazine* article was published in 2004, a brief piece for their weekly 'My Wheels' feature. I wrote about my Avensis 2-litre with Italian alloys that had just replaced a plain pencil-grey Nissan Primera which was for me a definite promotion on the car ownership ladder. Yes, I had to talk it up – the car *was* a Toyota – but it had air conditioning, Sony music system, cruise control, electric sunroof, beautiful metallic mauve paintwork, and a subtle rather than crass boy-racer rear spoiler. My prompt and ruse were the fact so-called friends and teaching colleagues at school had described its colour as pink. I recounted the marching of my A level English Literature group down to confront the Head of Art who instigated the colour ridicule, informing him and the class he was then teaching that the owner manual clearly stated the car's sophisticated hue as 'Chianti'.

The Rolling Stones at Hyde Park

Hyde Park, 1969; Weeley, 1971: I was at both. The first (the one people remember) is all rather vague as a memory, though certain aspects stand out – Paul, a school friend, arrived very late for our arranged meet at the A12 roundabout out of Ipswich for hitchhiking to London. However, that later start proved fortuitous as we were picked up by a Bedford van full of hippies who were also going and knew how to get there. I remember nothing of the drive and think we were politely left to ourselves. In London we parked somewhere not too far from Hyde Park, though this seems unlikely. I do recall there being a proverbial sea of people once at the famous venue and we never got anywhere near to even seeing the stage. And I only recall hearing a snatch of King Crimson's *21st Century Schizoid Man*, and definitely no Shelley poem read aloud or a single Stones song later on. We must have, yet nothing registers. But we were there! Paul and I would have been in our 5th year at school and I cannot believe we told either of our sets of parents the intention for that day: such cheeky subterfuge. The peak good fortune on that 5th of July, looking back, is how considerate and caring our Bedford van-load of hippies from Harwich were: when dropped off they told us if we met back at that spot, they'd take us to Ipswich on their way home. And we did. I don't know how, but we did. Our Stones stratagem was safely secured by the chance goodwill of meeting guys older than us, and who had some idea of the needs. Peace and Love.

Baseball Glove and Cap

The 'baseball' metaphor runs deep in American culture and my experience of playing the game in Germany. It was in the Little League and my team was the *Orioles*, a generic name (as well as obviously at Baltimore) and not linked to the Paul Revere Village army base where I also attended school aged 11 in 1965, or thereabouts. I played third base and pitched just the one time, this latter quite possibly a singular shared privilege for the sake of team spirit and individual aspiration. I also hit a home run, again just the once, but was given a dollar for doing so by the team coach – and without sullying the gesture with some thought of psychological intent, I think it was simply a friendly gesture, and quite likely a traditional one. I don't recall playing it for long, and never did football in a proper team, apart from on the concrete playground at a school I briefly attended in Omaha where it was tag/touch football and I do remember we were quite rough and tough at the scrimmage line, an unusual proclivity for me. So, there are fond memories of some national sports involvement and I was at least a part of that growing-up programme, though it did ultimately fail. But I still have the glove and cap on display at the top of a bookcase here at home after all those years, a metaphor for making roots that never quite took, yet dug around just enough to matter.

Orioles Little League baseball cap with glove

Vinyl

I had many sources over the years, most local and most charity shops: Oxfam used to be a favourite, especially in Sidmouth, but this organisation was one of the first wising up to the actual value of records; there were the Vinyl Exchange and Empire Exchange in Manchester, the second with its basement treasure trove of second-hand books and comics, albums industriously categorised, and 'adult material'; and I had one further excellent source somewhere on the southeast coast of England. I could get great buys from this latter, most at £3 each and all in superb condition. I can even remember times there, for example, when I'd be looking through the boxes on the floor and other people would come and go, gestures of commitment but really no more than lightweights. One guy would stop, look to his partner and suggest he was going to stay for a while so they should just move on, and he'd last about four minutes. Pathetic. You had to have stamina to search through box after box of relative crap to find something wanted. Occasional pearls inside the shells, at my price range anyway. I know there are bigger nerd vinyl buyers out there who range further for larger treasures. Each to their own. There were so many surprises in the complete unknowns, like the Herbie Mann's *Reggae* album including both Mick Taylor and Albert Lee on guitars. OK, I only listened the once, but I did actually see Albert Lee play Exmouth – of all the places – that one time too.

Speeches

The significance of a great speech passed me by in '63 –
sipping sodas to *Surfer Girl* in an Elk Horn café put a young
boy's mind on customised cars, first sex and an even more
distant beach, whereas the slow measure of Kennedy's *Ich
bin ein Berliner* or the intoning of King's *I had a dream*
would have to wait like treasure buried in the subconscious
and unearthed in some future recall. My small town then
was reality: older boys jerked off in abandoned rooms as I
turned away; ghosts in the haunted house made me run as
they mounted the stairs, and the locusts came in noisy
swarms then left their empty shells stuck to trees.
Discovering the fear in living with this meant more than
why in Saigon Thích Quảng Đức assumed the lotus position
and turned himself into a fireball, or how JFK's German
vision would disappear down a Dallas boulevard – and
looking back, it is the Beach Boy's innocence I miss.

Horror Story

The only Halloween I remember even vaguely from my childhood was in Norfolk, and in those days the real and imaginary scare was of razorblades inside popcorn balls, or LSD secreted into treats – here was the horror story in the 60s where kids in white sheets and carrying brown paper sacks walked neighbourhoods safely without parents and in the certain hope of bulging bags full of a different deadly. All these years later, and living in a country that has appropriated many of America's customs – like Halloween, but not, thankfully, endemic access to guns – I re-envisage those same streets: children and their armed escorts ready to shoot those unwilling to give to *their* rituals; how in these culture wars there will be checking for messages on the insides of candy wrappers (calls to worship an alternative god), or perhaps strange scared faces at curtains who, having inherited such new freedoms, are ignorant of a festivity's homespun danger. Unknowing might prompt a new horror, but at least call it American, and alien subliminals are unlike the domestic with its sugar and other sweet certainties of who they all are.

Little Wings

Her mother was crying because I played Karis' music, and this was bound to happen since she'd left home (although I think these songs were more like the ones I used to listen to when I was her age), but can you imagine the sobbing if Val had seen the kitchen door with condensation filming the glass and huge letters spelling *LITTLE WINGS* – a ghost of our daughter's handwriting from maybe months before – still there even after asking her to quit such scribbling because I suggested it was time she'd stopped behaving like a little girl?

Last Pear

While mowing the lawn in a late August afternoon I saw one of the only two pears that summer had fallen to the ground, shrivelled and browned having rotted there for days, with wasps flying in and out. I stopped cutting the grass immediately to pick the other still on its tree and took indoors to ask if she'd like a bite, but turning to me, Val declined. I therefore did instead, though it was actually too hard to eat. The previous year's tree had branches arced and hung low to the ground with all its fruit, but we naturally knew this following year's was limited to that pair, though I checked again and again to be sure, not quite believing there could be such a difference. Mowing once more on the other side of the tree, I found a third, this obviously the one I knew as being from the brace because it was in the same state and probably only fallen that day, wasps walking on but not inside. After that much looking I'd missed not an abundance but more all the same.

VIP at The Rolling Stones, Wembley

To confirm, I've seen them twice: that one technically non-visual performance in 1969, and then in 1995 for the *Voodoo Lounge* tour gig at Wembley. This was special not just because it was fully sighted – and it *was* the Stones – but because the family and I were VIP guests. I concede it could be argued this is an exaggeration as we were actually VIP parking guests, but this is more than most attending that day could say. We'd gone to the Freddie Mercury Memorial Concert at Wembley in '92 (Ana, a member of the Queen fan club, getting tickets), and having arrived very early, waiting hours and then suffering a delayed entry because of stadium incompetence – missing the beginning – I responded the next day as I always did in such circumstances: I wrote a strongly worded letter of complaint. And it worked. Although I said in my letter I'd never attend the national stadium again, I was offered first entry into any future performance there along with VIP parking to compensate for our poor experience. So, when the Stones' gig was announced, I pounced. One of my favourite English teaching lessons was the 'letter of complaint', firstly polite but firm, and if no success in response to this, a second more strident tone to follow. And all had to be presented precisely to my guidelines on a formal letter structure, with modes of address matched precisely by modes of closure. Over a lifetime I had many refunds and apologies and token gifts of recompense on the strength of my own letters. Though I really can't remember all the letters and 'successful' responses – there were so many – my favourite was a replacement pair of Dr. Martens boots when I had complained their 'Guaranteed for Life' soles had not withstood one year of mucking out the pigs at the farm where I worked. The company's *For Life* guarantee has, by the way, subsequently been withdrawn, though this was in 2018 and not back around 1978 when I'd written my letter detailing the acidic nature of a pig's urinary system and output, and how any conceivable impact of this was definitely covered within the 'non-industrial abuse' stricture of their policy as mine was an agricultural and natural working environment.

Basketball Hoot

On arrival as the all-American boy at my English secondary modern school in 1967, I had many *specialist* experiences, not least the apocalypse of discovering 'school uniform' for the first time when I appeared dressed for an Ivy League fashion convention. In curriculum terms, I was placed in two top sets – Maths, from where I quickly tumbled to a fourth set CSE group and eventually attained CSE Grade 4 so a symmetry of mathematical sorts, and English where the teacher kept me for the duration as a sustained challenge to my national traits. I also experienced The Phenomenon of Alternative Histories: having just covered the American War of Independence during a brief grade-school spell in Omaha, learning about the ridiculous English fighting in cumbersome tight formations wearing brightly coloured formal uniforms, I was then taught at Chantry in Ipswich about the appalling tactics of the Americans fighting in camouflaged clothes and ambushing British soldiers by springing out at them from behind trees and other concealing shrubberies. Most absurd was the Head of PE who on my arrival insisted I joined the school's basketball team that was doing well, even beating the Americans from a nearby army base school, who was crestfallen when I eventually persuaded him I had never played the game as a kid – apart from shooting the occasional hoops in a school playground in Germany, this disorientating his geographical expectations even further.

The Disappearance of Vinyl

Albums disappeared from my cottage at Belstead in the mid-70s. They were taken to sell by a friend I let stay for a short while, and among the number stolen was Jimi Hendrix's *Are You Experienced,* a significant loss to me. He also purloined two eponymous LPs, though this is unlikely the reason for their taking: the albums *Yes* and *Black Sabbath,* the second of special importance because I'd bought it at Portabella Road Market in London, and the other personal stories connected to it. That album would also be worth money today – not to sell, but a further value in my collection. Not necessarily worse, but different, I also personally disappeared albums before this. In the early days of my move to England in '67 I had a few soul albums: the Tamla Motown *Four Tops - Greatest Hits*, the Atlantic compilation *This is Soul,* and the Atlantic *The Exciting Wilson Pickett* with its bright pink cover. I disappeared these because I had discovered Hendrix and immediately bought my precious *Are You Experienced* and became psychedelicised. With transformations occurring in my new life at school, and a growing love for any and all 'underground' music, I did what most teenagers do in finding an allegiance, and pettily shifted prior affiliations – I think literally throwing rather than giving away those soul albums. But *what does not change / is the will to change* and I did also see in Ipswich, back again in the 70s, Sister Sledge, The Detroit Spinners, The Stylistics, David Ruffin and Hot Chocolate. Growing up was an enigmatic business.

30+ Years

Teaching in the same school for thirty years gives one a privileged and fundamental perception of a local characteristic and personality – this I apply broadly and fondly and respectfully to all the students I taught, as well as colleagues. Perhaps I'll try to expand on this another time, but it is a complex absorption to describe. Similar but easier to articulate because it is a more focused encounter, 35+ years as an examiner of GCSE English Literature gives one a unique perspective on students more generally, or to be precise, nationally. Before examining went online and the marking therefore randomised, students' work came physically from a single school for which an examiner was wholly responsible (and it was also then a number of schools per examiner), so you could gain a strong sense of each school's teaching approaches, its 'academic' range, its cultural and social foundations – this would be obvious and dynamic – its ethos and so much more. A school's choice of texts for study could also be telling, but over many years and on a national basis there were two clear, popular choices: *Of Mice and Men* and *An Inspector Calls*. There are many reasons for this, so, for example, good storytelling, accessibility, meaningfulness, teaching preference and the accumulated resources any teacher/school would have for that selection. As an examiner, it took a certain kind of resilience to read the 400th response to *Of Mice and Men* and know you must treat that commentary with the attention and freshness it deserved. The contradiction was that Curley's wife only wore so much red to signal danger as well as sexuality, and she had a finite number of sausage curls hanging meatily or metaphorically about her interpretable face, but each time such details were reported and explored there was an individual start point to that long and indefinite lineage of answering. This wonderful problem for that text ended in 2015 when the then Education Secretary Michael Gove had all American authors banned from GCSE English Literature examination and therefore study. This was an appalling though not surprising act of curriculum vandalism – as well as destructive individual whim – and it was ironically countered by all those other texts (often certain poems) whose themes and storylines also focused on humanity's frailties and cruelties and injustices. These too at times portrayed explorations of an individual's catastrophic personal errors with, usually, a hope for and perhaps attainment of redemption. Students always responded then and do so now empathetically to J.B. Priestley's message about social and economic injustice as well as the personal challenges this caused. For example, in 2011 when the wealthiest in the UK had their banking practices exposed, this was a contemporary resource with which to engage and use to relate; and the Grenfell disaster of 2017 provided, as I vividly recall, a palpable sense of how privation and disenfranchisement was as rampant then as in the world of Priestley's play. Of course, literature provides that 'safe' if nonetheless relevant remove for reflection on the here and now. Living in a democracy, there isn't any censorship, though there are paradoxes, and the irony.

Danmark På Prærien

Velkommen to flaeskesteg, rullepolse, skinke, and to a prairie's past pickled in a waft of Elk Horn's Danish windmill sails; to kringle and dansk lagkage, to my grandparents' home still on 173, to Lutherans and licorice, to VikingHjem and Andersen's tales, to cherry bombs and chicken heads, and to prairie grass waves. Velkommen to Carlson, my mother Aasta May, to smørrebrød, aeblskiver, medisterpolse, and to Exodus and grandpa's Elim Children's Home, to flora Danica and blue fluted, to my one-time højskole, to rock fights and burning a farm down – nearly – to grandma's kyllingesteg, to Alma, Emery and Glenn, to Aasta Schack and Axel and all of us, to 98.7% English only (and Danish declining), to 76.7% who drove alone, and to grandpa's slow smooth safe drive into town. Velkommen to a Blended Service of the Eucharist and easy-to-follow old-songs-sung-in-an-upbeat style, to *Snagajob* at Walnut, Atlantic, Kirkman, Avoca, Exira, Harlan and Shelby all only 10-15 miles from Elk Horn where there are no offers; to empty bourbon bottles in grandpa's barn, to no school on Friday so Spartan fans can cheer girls' basketball, to Danes and Lady Danes who still drift across the years in EHS and lessons learned in the colours of change, to pickled Red Cabbage and Red Beets in jars, and to finding and now.

John and Robin

Both 15, maybe 16, John was 6 foot plus definitely more and Robin was probably 'just' 6 foot. I was smaller. Both were on the Chantry School basketball team that I never joined, and they were good. John also played the trumpet and he appeared on a couple of the songs I recorded and sent to another friend Paul's uncle who worked in the 'music industry' in London though he never replied or returned the cassette tape. John, Robin and I would dress up in smart suits with waistcoats and those shirts with extraordinarily large collars in the late 60s – with ties – and because of their height we swaggered to the pubs together to drink lager and play darts. At least two of us would usually smoke cigarillos and we were the bee's knees for underage drinking when looking so cool and smooth. Obviously, the pub owners then couldn't give a toss and simply ignored the fact we were obviously overdressed and overconfident 15 or 16 year olds drinking a few pints, playing some darts and never causing any kind of problems that would make anyone else care either.

Imposters ready for a night out

Music Club

At the civic college where I took A levels, a student's timetable had to be complemented with something other than 'academic' studies. One year I added woodwork, which I had enjoyed at Chantry – making there a lamp with a round base and oval middle shaped on a wood turning lathe. I'd also made a 'checkerboard' effect bowl of contrasting coloured woods – and I therefore made a bowl again, but a simpler design with a single block of wood, yet a quality one, screwed to a base to mount on a lathe for the external rounding and hollowing out of the inside. However, I cut too deep and exposed the screws at the base from the inside, ruining it. That is until the lecturer showed me how to make a design out of the error by filling the screw holes with another darker coloured wood, adding further filled holes to match, and sanding/lathing this flat and smooth to what looked like a cleverly intended circle pattern. The other complementary lesson I attended was at a college annexe and this was Music Club where we simply listened to songs played from various records and all genres by the college Music lecturer who was also obviously having his timetable worked to meet whatever requirements there were imposed for these *other* (enjoyable as they turned out) activities. He also invited any of those attending to bring in their own music – vinyl albums as it was early 70s – and we could introduce these ourselves and talk about them. Of course, I eagerly obliged. I may well have been the only one, annoyingly so for others who I don't recollect wanted to be there, and thus my keenness galled and perhaps they also thought my enthusiasm meant the course continued. I forget the range of albums I did bring in over the duration, but I do know one was the 1966 Buddy Rich *Swingin' New Big Band* – I'd recently discovered jazz – and I had the lecturer play the album's great *West Side Story*

Medley track, this recorded live like all the others and full of sass as well as the swing, which no doubt I talked about in my introducing the album. I know I had this habit of moving my hand to the rhythmic shifts of the music – in this class done down by my seated side, though ostentatiously visible to all those behind, whereas at live gigs it would rock all over the performing place – and it was a pretentious affectation that no doubt got plenty of sneers and other mockery from the majority there at Music Club as I of course always sat at the front, being so keen. I still have and play the Buddy Rich occasionally – it is sensational – and shortly after my mother's passing in 2005, I was sent to have for myself that genuinely beautiful checkerboard bowl I had made for her and she kept all that time.

Olin

It is perfectly natural to ask myself: what if I had met my
father Olin, lived with him a while, called him Stan or
Swede like his friends, grew up with those big hands I was
told he had and personally know from occasionally wearing
his wedding ring on my thumb (that other woman's, who
kindly sent to me as a memento), put his in mine like fathers
do, as sentimental and annoying as that sounds; and if I
watched him work on a Chevy, handing down tools
probably barked for with my only ever knowing then as
much as I do these days about cars; and if I saw him going
off to work at school teaching other young boys he'll
obviously have known better than me how to tune an engine
or smooth out a scar; and if he observed the patterns for my
job exploring the mechanics of words, finding some point
where I begin; and if I listened to the dreams he must have
had, different to mine, talked about all that love or whatever
it was he shared around too much that I wouldn't
understand then and still don't today, because as a ladies'
man I'd guess he spread his much too thin?

First Time at Portman Road, Ipswich Town FC

This was my first time at any English football game, early 70s. I couldn't believe it – standing only. *Everyone* standing! Not just this: you would be watching in one position at a certain moment, and the next you would be in an entirely different place, swept there by the mass wave of an ever-changing crowd celebrating a goal or berating en masse a referee or opposition player. I don't think I was by this stage still the all-American boy with a 'superior' standard of expectation, but I was an American who even in 60s USA had always had an individual seat for watching a sports game. And men were pissing along the corrugated iron walls at the top back of the North Stand where I was. And the police were there, grabbing you like a criminal when you had been catapulted into them by one of those seismic crowd shifts. Though I was never a regular, I later became an appalling lout, turning up drunk and aggressive on the few occasions I still went to a game; my visit to the lion's den at Norwich was another one where I await self-Karma's comeback on my outrageous behaviour that night. Now, I confess, a peripheral if still loyal supporter – you do not lose that connection – I was blessed to be a part of the wonderful Bobby Robson era, enjoying the team's success under his management, feeling close when a Chantry classmate married one of the star players, and sticking it to Arsenal in the 1978 FA Cup so I could do the same to the Gunners-supporting mobile butcher who delivered sausages to our house when I was farming in the Chilterns.

Sad Lisa and a Harvest Touch

Val broke up with me sometime during or soon after an evening at hers, listening to Cat Stevens, and the last track I heard before leaving was *Sad Lisa* I think, though this is likely imagined and linked to my deep sense of misery as well as prompted by the song's plaintive storyline. This feeling of loss transmuted into a general emotional malaise for the weeks that followed – not a teenagers' morose incomprehension, but a more mature, experienced pathos – and I would go to pubs to obviously drink bucket-loads (a classic to fuel rather than ease the pain) and add to my maudlin mainlining by constantly listening to Harry Nilsson's *Without You* which seemed to be on every juke box at that time, or perhaps knowingly only the ones in the pubs I targeted for my pathetic self-destruction. Not that long after the break-up, in December 1972, I went to see Barclay James Harvest play at the Ipswich Civic College Main Hall, and I was standing on my own doing that ridiculous *thing* of using my hand and arm to plot the rhythms of the music (and thinking about this, it must have been a copying of Joe Cocker at Woodstock, as seen in the film) when I felt someone come up behind, wrap their arms around my chest and give me a hug. It was Val, my hand-gymnastics remarkably achieving a better kind of thing, though she does remind me it was actually my wearing of that pale-blue towelling shirt with the feel of velvet that was a call to our getting back together again.

Mr Webber

Informed later of his visit, at the time I was unaware when the Headmaster came into our school hall to observe me, eyes closed in reverie, rubbing up and down a support pole on stage. He walked back out immediately. I was thrusting my guitar across the upright like a bottleneck, Sam and I having been given permission to use the hall's sound system to practise our music. We were anarchically loud, indulging in a wild jam, with Sam amped up on his flute and my searching out any weird sounds I could produce in lieu of having expensive devices like fuzz or wah-wah to hand. I'm sure my actions were of some concern to Mr Webber, but suspect it was the noise that drove him away – he was a remarkably tolerant and supportive person and quite simply won't have enjoyed what we were performing. I first met Mr Webber with my parents at an interview for joining Chantry Secondary Modern fresh from Omaha via Germany and totally ill-prepared for the culture shock. I remember politely responding with 'yeah' to his many enquiries, being corrected after each with 'we say *yes* here'. It was a little intimidating, but there was another layer to the advice I didn't understand at that time. Throughout my two and a half years at Chantry there were many personal occasions when he displayed the depths of his forbearance as well as thoughtfulness. For example, I once crafted a pottery dish where, with the guidance of my superb Art teacher, I'd used brightly coloured vinyl/ceramic shapes to decorate its face so when fired these would melt into random, psychedelic patterns. I loved it. However, I was later told I couldn't take it home because Mr Webber had already appropriated it for display in his Headmaster's office. Angered, I didn't exactly confront him but arranged a meeting where he explained how pleased and proud he was of my dish, wanting to keep it as a showcase of student work, buying it from me at his suggested price of £5 – quite a bit of money at that time. I was naturally delighted with his comments and the compulsory purchase. Another more remarkable gesture concerned a school magazine Sam and I produced using facilities provided by the school. We titled it *Fink*, and sold it at school to raise money for a charity. The contents were mainly poems and song lyrics with occasional opinion pieces, all quite forthright in their political radicalism and teenage revolutionary ideas. Quite naïve of course, but genuinely felt. The problem was that teachers had complained to Mr Webber about the magazine's 'propaganda', especially considering the fact it was produced within the school. Sam and I were summoned to his office and informed of this criticism. Mr Webber explained he'd understood entirely why staff had objected, and expressed his own disagreement with most of what we had written. He also argued that we at least 'weren't cabbages' and instead praised our having firmly held views and expressing them. He concluded he'd therefore ignore the staff grievance, and I do think I fully sensed the gravity of such a decision in our favour at that time. *Yes*, I am sure I did.

First Time, Second Time Around

There are a number of musicians I never got to see in their prime but have since in the latter phase or twilight of their careers. These are James Taylor, Yusuf Islam (Cat Stevens), The Isley Brothers, Arthur Lee's Love, Wishbone Ash (both ongoing versions), Crosby, Stills and Nash, Roy Harper, John Etheridge solo and in a modern Soft Machine line-up, Tír na nÓg (they were at Weeley but I'm sure I was sleeping at the time), Bert Jansch with John Renbourn, Johnny Winter, Albert Lee, Peter Green, Paul Rogers, The Doobie Brothers, Michael Chapman, Stan Webb, and Neil Young. I will mention the Freddie Mercury Memorial Concert again where I saw David Bowie and Elton John. I also got to see Conway Twitty at the Siskiu State Fair (Yreka) in 1992, taking my 12-year-old daughter, and *I* certainly had a great time. There are a further few who deserve to be mentioned though 'removed' from their original bands, like Ginger Baker with his Jazz Confusion, and Robin Williamson without any of the other Incredible String Band. In other fringe contexts I saw Roger Daltrey and Gary Brooker. I did most recently from these subsidiary categories see The Groundhogs, although the only remaining original member was drummer Carl Stocks so I don't think this counts, as incendiary as they were then. I haven't included Gene Simmons singing the American national anthem at the Wembley NFL Vikings/Steelers game in 2013, or any performers I saw in their prime but also subsequently. I only got weepily emotional seeing CS&N, me never a singalong kinda guy, but trying with opening numbers *Carry On* and *Questions* I did choke, hit by a passing freight train of nostalgia. None of the later-in-life performances were ever naff, often seeming as fresh as ever – I felt then and still do now that James Taylor's vocal matures with age – and/or bands often have session players/singers bolstering sounds to verisimilitudes of the past, this often including their children all grown up and additions to the groups. Peter Green played with less pace than in his heyday but was nonetheless mesmerising, and Johnny Winter was similar – another fine guitarist playing with him to add occasional background oomph – though Johnny's slide could still glide. The only one who was at times hard to take in a new incarnation was Stan Webb, formerly of Chicken Shack, his set existential and chaotic at times – though also sublime, especially his distinctive vocal – and if he ever had been PC in inclination this was clearly anathema to him now. One other more comic indication of a past catching up was Arthur Lee and Love playing the Phoenix at Exeter, and when Lee strutted up to the mic to begin the gig with that enthusiastic, shouted clichéd line (or similar) of 'Hey, how's it going....' he turned to the bass player and you could just hear him asking '...where are we?'

A Whispering

The fallen leaves were birds lifting heads in the wind and I could also see a snake jump out of the ground – it was absurd, so easily deceived, and I asked myself if these were a consequence of flashbacks or age. Karis and a friend were older too, but spiralled happily down a twisting slide in the park I had brought them to; and from my car, out of the cold, I continued to watch the metamorphosing, watched these girls for a moment who were not embarrassed by playing. Perhaps it was reading Brodsky on imminent death, how he could *hear each moment whisper as it slides by,* and I was trying to play like the other children who hadn't yet had to listen but knew of this acceptance: one day, one day…

Gants Hill Hitchhiking

Hitching from London back to Ipswich in the late 60s through the 70s, I would always start from Gants Hill where the A12 began. There was also a pub nearby that served a cheap and tasty pint of mild and I would have two or three before starting the journey home – the bladder of youth a resilient organ. Hitching was common and safe, maybe not inherently, yet seemed genuinely so and I only ever had a few problematic encounters. There was the occasional threatening behaviour – the point of such a bullying person picking someone up being to exercise that power over their captive audience – but the only seriously dangerous moment I experienced was with the driver who while racing his sports car along the dual carriageway, rolled up a fag at the same time, using his knees to steady the steering wheel. Listening to Springsteen's 2019 song *Hitch Hikin'*, I recognise my exhibitionist cigarette guy in the Boss's 'Gearhead' who 'wants to show a kid what this thing'll do'; when Bruce sings how the 'Family man gives me a ride', I think of that one who with his car already full of wife and kids picks me up as another one, and they all sing their Christian hymns while I politely listen in, and I am driven all the way home to my cottage door, their kindness more than words of faith in a song. There were so many rides up and down to London but also the music gigs and festivals, and it is impossible to recall the journeys as they merge into the one anonymous means of getting from A to B these all ultimately were. It was the regular hitching from Kesgrave back to my Belstead home where I got the fullest range of experience. There *were* the sexual predators, and being a bloke, it just so happens mine were gay, usually leaving it to suggesting/sounding out, apart from the GI from the local American base who so aggressively mentioned that I was 'lucky' he hadn't 'jumped' me. My one regular was a wonderful driver and drive, and I would leave Val's house in the evening to hopefully catch him on his way to his nightshift job. Nothing like the 'souped-up '72' of Bruce Springsteen's Gearhead, this man drove a black 1962 Wolesley as steadily as he was with his minimal conversation – just enough to be honest and direct – and it never seemed like a commitment he felt he had to make having picked me up that first time, and of course he will have been aware of my regular timings. I must have known his name then, but that's gone now. But what hasn't faded is the memory of his kindness and the sense of security on my way to getting home.

My Running

My first proper run was an early morning organised three-mile team race, which our trio lost badly, and my personal manifestation of the consequence was a momentary, slight lapse in the control of my bladder and then a celebratory can of beer. It was later when growing in distances I bought Walsh shoes from Kendal, putting an end to shin splints that felt like snakebites. Preparing for a full marathon meant squeezing the training in between a day job and marking students' work late at night, or occasionally at school during long Devon lunchtime sessions – out past hillbilly farms and their contrasting sweet views across deep valleys. Weekends back home might be a Sunday Fartlek up on the local school's running track. Then there was the lament of the meniscus tear; and when this had fully healed that first twenty-mile group run. I'll never understand how I would always prefer going up and up the hills, but it will have happened when distance was no longer a number and there was a lyricism in the rhythm of a stride. If only I hadn't lost my running diary, a chronicle of tuned-in wild words and not an *endorphin* written in any ecstatic lines, but the certainty of euphoric endogenous opioids. For the marathon, 1983, my running partners and I had team vests, I hit my wall at something like twenty-two miles to walk for a little while, finished in six and a half minutes under 4 hours, but there was no Vaseline for me, thank you.

Val and Ana were unable to get to the race, or so I thought: they'd hitched a ride in, and I only knew they were there as I crossed the finish line!

On Our Own Break

We arrived on our own without any other family members and without friends, so just the two of us, and not to be private or romantic, necessarily, so not *not* to be either of these, but when we entered the lodge our dining table had been laid for six people with elaborate place settings of designer plates and bowls, the wine glasses ready too – even all three of the bedrooms had six bath towels neatly placed on beds with individual soaps put in fancy-folded smaller ones for display – and being a couple obviously means you are not alone, but can be, and the owners of the place we had rented might have checked who was coming, just in case.

Photographs

Photographs were framed and always placed neatly above where I would write – two full bookshelf lines – though I have now moved by the window to look out on the front lawn and beyond, East Hill in the distance before things were built in my eye-line, like how there is always change. Those photos were set against a handful received by post one day: my family's organised rows in contrast to that clutch of images, some from fifty years before. A father was seen for the first time, one black-and-white snap where his arms were wrapped around a four year old daughter, then the full colour captures of his wife, the other son, and that sister much older, still being held; his hand-built custom cars too, and even an ultralight to pilot solo into the freedom of the sky, but it was also no surprise that after all those years, his first son, as far as I now knew, wasn't in a single shot, or as his last wife confirmed when sending these, he never told her that I had been.

Stan with Bobbie Ann

Perambulation

I found an air-conditioned place to sit, comfortable chair, a half-decent magazine, and reading about the *Perambulation of the Town Leat* – this medieval custom of water-bailing in Tiverton – I heard the increasing grumbles of someone approaching up the corridor to my side. I assumed it was the pace of his or her stride in this place where all can only dream of joining in a procession, when he slowly rounded the open door in a wheelchair, each semi-turn of the wheels a different struggle in staccato sounds. Val was elsewhere in the building getting her own advice, and when she appeared with the walker but on her own two feet, I lifted her up, so to speak, and made a run for our lives into the street.

Popping Evan Williams

Pulling the cork top on the bottle of Evan Williams Single Barrel, it popped – being two thirds gone – and echoed in the empty dining room next door, glancing off the new oak laminate to be absorbed in the still drying plaster of the walls: that space, when finished, where I would be drinking much more in the time I still had to waste, as happily. Its old carpet had been there for nearly thirty-five years, and even at its start was second-hand at the Oxford flat, so it too would have seen plenty of drift and deterioration over its bourbon days. The room was gutted, cleared for renovation, but also the Feng Shui of imagining fresh beginnings, returning only those things necessary for nostalgia to feel reconciled with what it had abandoned. Like the scent sniffed as a boy from the empties of Grandpa's whiskey among the stripped corncob fuel in his barn, there was a memory that would remain, and it would still make noises like that ricochet in the shell of its boom.

The Importance of Music in 1971: 2

America's eponymous debut album seemed curious in being launched on the back of their seminal hit single *A Horse With No Name* and yet this track didn't appear on it. The reality is this isn't the exact chronology of that release: it came out initially in 1971 to apparently only moderate success, but after recording some additional material, including the then *Desert Song* – latter renamed *AHWNN* after going down well in live performance – it was re-released in 1972 with the song included and going to number 1 in the United States. That didn't make any difference to me. I already had the first release as I bought it soon after radio play of *A Horse...* here in England, where the three main band members lived, but obviously before the re-release. It became an instant favourite and a song filling then and full now of poignant memories encompassing falling in love – I probably should just leave it there as a finite romantic observation – but also all of the other paraphernalia attached to growing up in the early 70s. The three core members of Gerry Beckley, Dewey Bunnell and Dan Peek were living at an American Air Force base in West Ruislip, London – attending London Central High School – and I felt I had an affinity with them, also an American living in England, and the comparisons stretch even further from there: I listened to great music; America made it. Their musical map was plotted on the geography of west coast harmony a la Crosby, Stills and Nash, but it is a definable enough terrain. Beckley and Bunnell have distinctive vocals, and indeed continued as the band after Dan Peek left in 1977 (he passed away in 2011), and their songwriting and acoustic guitar playing are idiosyncratic within this expansive genre. *A Horse With No Name* is the fifth track on the re-release and it is the simplest of acoustic strumming with a melody line that is almost monosyllabic over a driving beat up to the memorable chorus. What carries it there, of course, are the obtuse but mesmerising lyrics, the *la la, la la la la* harmonising providing a hiatus for reflection on what has been intoned by the ungrammatical storytelling of *there ain't no one for to give you no pain*: screw double negatives if it scans. The transformation of the desert to sea, the significance of *nine days*, the release of the horse, the exhausted naming that ends up observing *things*, and humans, that are loveless – it is a wondrous landscape of meaningless words creating meaning if we just listen and absorb. The album ends on the *Pigeon Song* which I have always liked and sung aloud for the sinister nonsense of its hillbilly nihilism: *Well I had me a pigeon / By the name of Fred / But I done shot him / In the head // Had me a railroad / Down on the ridge / But I done blowed up / The bridge // Had me a dog / He was my best friend / But to him / I done put an end // Had me a farm / Sittin' pretty on the hill / But if you look / It ain't there still // I don't know why I done it / Honest it ain't like me / But I ain't sad now I done it / 'Cause a baby boy has got to be free.*

Moles

I was never a natural killer of animals. I mean as an American of course. I didn't grow up with guns, didn't go hunting, and never had Sunday dinner with Charlton Heston carving the roast with his cold dead hands. I did some stupid things with cherry bombs and once shot a fledgling blackbird through a nest with a BB gun, but I was showing off for others who got a kick out of this when I did not. Years later, all grown up with a job and a family and a home and a lawn, things changed. The moles came. Their blind devotion to digging and signposting routes with marker mounds of soil drove me to stalk them on tip-toe, considering how to kill: standing absolutely still, I'd shovel one out whole (if lucky), otherwise, just stab with knife and fork, whatever was to hand. Things had changed dramatically. An English teacher by then, at school my students read *Lord of the Flies* and I taught Golding's warning of our inhumanity. Their innocence was a comfortable temptation, but the moles just returned again and again. I developed skills and used esoteric approaches researched online: empty bottles, chewing gum, children's miniature plastic windmills, stink/smoke bombs, and a hosed car's exhaust fumes were all directed via varying placements into their tunnels. I also wrote a clutch of poems about the ongoing battlegrounds, literally and only sometimes philosophically. All these years later, moles continue to come and go, and the contemporary world has turned Golding into an historian of the ordinary. I now set designated traps, plotting routes to and fro, and manage the damage as best I can to themselves and me. My final mole poem is yet to be written.

CT and the KKK

It might seem it would be easier for me to write about my growing-up love for 60s/70s rock, folk, progressive rock, soul and the rest, compared to a later-life enthusing about Conway Twitty and Country and Western. I should stress I'm no fan of redneck C&W, but Christian Country can be sublime, although it is clear that pedal steel is an instrument gifted from The Lamenting Deities, and *whippoorwill* is a word as countrified as *Hank*. Conway Twitty is a name rooted in C&W World, and his R&R birthing is just another route along the way – *It's Only Make Believe* was released in 1958 so I was 4 years old, but at some stage in my incipient musical absorption that song with its ascending melodramatic song-structure and delivery blew me away. I have two significant later favourites from him: *I See the Want to in Your Eyes* and *There's A Honky Tonk Angel*. These and CT's singing epitomise all that is fundamental in this genre – the pain, suffering and longing of love and its heartfelt with-any-twang-going vocal representation. 'I could light that fire again' Conway threatens to the angel and then asks 'how strong is a band of gold?' A simple and familiar enough lyrical soap-opera, but he adds 'How many women just like you have silent schemes; how many men like me do they sleep with in their dreams?' Mischa Scorer and Wayne Carson wrote those raunchy rhetorical lines, but like any affecting performer, CT gives them their credible drama. When I connected this song's title with my poem about seeing the Ku Klux Klan, it wasn't a Conway Twitty symbiotic link, but quite simply the year 1974 when I juggled both.

National Curriculum at Sea Life

Karis would be seven when spring began, and that day she read beautifully of *aquaria* and *anemones*, watery new words from a brochure to bathe and prepare her for hot summer SATs that tested within landlocked and fixed boundaries – unable to reward 'the *o* flying away from didn't is an apostrophe', or to understand, as it was only October, the other beauty of her error when reading the 'astonishing angels' from which everything at Sea Life could be seen. Most notable *angles* are actually hard, as she'd learn and tell herself one day when discovering what might have been.

Recycling

We were maybe half a mile away, returning home from shopping, and there dancing in the middle of the road – a random, manic but clearly enthusiastic and self-amusing jig – the bin-man was wearing a crushed, tan straw hat as he carried a recycling bag back to the house from where he had cavorted it to his lorry. The hat was once hers and earlier that morning had been in our own big green sack, and even though Val was sitting next to me I knew she would not want to see this, as I personally always somehow had to, noting that here was a moment's illumination of an alternative life being lived.

Soft Jazz and Snow

She was living in Talent, Oregon, knowingly unwell at the time, and I visited my mother there twice before she passed. One day I sat in the living room with her, soft jazz playing and her sleeping on the easy chair, feet dreaming a long walk. There was a cottonwood snowfall at that last of May, the snag of flakes on cobwebs, garden furniture, and the saplings raising their hopes for a future. Ends and beginnings were everywhere. I decided I would take a walk and connect myself to the wider view within that 'older persons' community of homes, and perhaps also a momentary sense of a differing ease. Making a circuit along its street, I met Jack and his wife: Jack with enormous hands he called *too grubby* from plumbing and garden chores to shake mine – and there was a tell-tale grass stain on his jeans' knee – when all of a sudden *He's got leukaemia* she told me. It was probably a week after this I had to travel back home, but soon enough across such a distance I returned. So now on a late August morning, I was combing and styling my hair when she began to turn away from a hard life – me making my vain arrangements for the day – and from that moment there were no more words or looks, and whatever had been said would have to do, forever. Having travelled all those miles once more to hold her hand and to say goodbye, this was the most domestic of ends; I did not see her retreat but only my face in the misted mirror and what I could hear of the others. There were more days before I was bereft; more days for me to groom before I left.

Set Solid

The things you built as a father – trying your best – many or most must come to an end, and there was such a day for the second and good rabbit run. The first did not keep a killer dog out which snapped at and punctured her bunny's lung (yet there is a place that can last, where they are all eventually buried and a sentimental rose-bush planted above). But this better protection and home that housed Karis' others and last one – then ours when she left home – had taken minutes to pull from the ivy and overgrown grass, its wood rotted and the Armadillidium spilling out from their residence. All but that main post had been concreted in to secure the gate and provide its central support, a pillar bolstered further with broken brick and stone, whatever I could muster at the time to help and hold. It was set solid, though also tested and old.

No Suspension of Disbelief

It was during the summer break when vandals disguised as suspended ceiling fitters got into my classroom and destroyed it with their installation. I hadn't been told of this and therefore hadn't removed the music posters and pictures covering most of my ceiling, including a section dedicated to C&W. Those on walls were also part-covered or ripped by the 'improvements', including ones given as leaving gifts by students, and others collected over many years, including my own school days. I was in enraged disbelief to discover, informing the Headmaster of a likely resignation, but was ignored because of my renowned volatility: this true and often on spontaneous display or in performance precisely because of that renown. I remained in post, deciding to completely cover the sound-proofing tiles with replacement pictures, which I did, leaving the originals as a concealed protest and where students leaving in the future could write private messages, which they did, some rude. The music posters and pictures were an expression of me in my classroom – a place for all others to convey who they were. An initial visual distraction, my students would soon move beyond this and absorb that personal statement, and I know from their comments over the years how engaged they were with that demonstration of self. After I retired, new buildings were built, and my classroom – a portacabin – was moved to the Foreign Languages area for their use, recent pictures removed, but the originals intact and still speaking of a presence before its eventual demise.

Distant

I have been distant most of my life – actual miles, unknowing, in new narratives. Memory and discovery fight it out and find it out, clarity that survives, haze, a retelling that glosses or grazes. Miles first then: family and home, roots as anchor, moves not chosen soon enough are; a lizard crawled across to leave alternative trails. The unknowing is a secret – partially seen – then waiting for its doors to open wide. Storytelling is prose dressed as lyric sung by the drunk and the Lorelai, various lines recalled. A life lived by this kind of précis gets to the gist like the exercise it is, and the divide *is* linear if drawing as the illusion of having arrived. Unable to attend, these are reasons why, and distances retold still are.

Leave

Later in the morning of the day she left to fly home to America – this reversal in our lives and domiciles – it was relatively good for me, but not her, my walking in to our town, November-crisp and a clear blue sky with sun shining, passing by that one other thing she had wanted to see – too late then with her nearing the long flight back home as I was still on my feet – such an enormous new-build of older people's apartments to dwarf the thatched restaurant by its side and those houses directly opposite the stream, their years of a beautiful view she'll once have seen also completely destroyed. The new walls of red brick will never be pretty like the fallen autumn leaves on that footbridge over the river when I returned home, so many still fresh, if pastel, and the few a vibrant orange, or as I still saw that bright colour of her hair, though now gone.

The End

I recently entered an international poetry competition with a found prose poem in three parts titled *On Significant Endings* and it was written in response to the theme 'Post Apocalypse'. It is not unusual for a writer to produce recurring themes/references, and mine are common enough ones like politics and religion, personal identity, personal experience – especially the link between past and present – and contemporary matters that can and do intrude at the time of writing. A found poem will be similarly sourced on occasions, but it generally takes a theme that is researched online and pieced together, that crafting process, with the information and ideas discovered. So for this work I found, among much else used, a reference to Sommarøy, a northern Norwegian island where its 350 inhabitants collectively agreed to end the notion of time; the Verloren Hoop, a Dutch phrase meaning 'last troop': soldiers going to their end in a final battle; the imaging of a supermassive black hole; diagnostic gastroscopy duration; the doomsday clock, and my own prompted phrase 'Sacrifice is the same in any language' that the judge selected as a 'gut punch of a line' which I rather liked as an observation. In its third section *The First Twelve Minutes of Technology* there is a line which is 'An ideal video lesson lasting 8-12 minutes leaves no room for *Woodstock* or *Easy Rider*' and this is another one of those personal interventions, here referring both to the four-part lesson plan ideology I suffered during the later part of teaching career, and then to the two films I would show my GCSE English groups at the end of their studies when this was 100% coursework and therefore no terminal exams. It was an opportunity naturally to entertain, to celebrate my personal past, to explore those anxieties and dreams I had as a teenager and how this was on the one hand linked to music and on the other hand to notions of personal choice and freedom, as fatalistic as that was in one of the films. This eventually stopped as times changed: there was no longer an ending to a course with instead looming terminal examinations and thus no prospect for a wind-down moment – especially with pressures on them and me and the school for a results-driven focus – and their own collective interests as teenagers moved too far beyond the links we used to find with mine. There was also the issue of both films being rated 18, and though the students were all able to access materials far more 'rateable' as such themselves, and obviously did, I wasn't prepared to risk my professional end by continuing to show them.

Manchester

My 35+ years of examining GCSE English Literature took place each summer, starting at home in the 80s and initially with physical papers – thousands of them – then online from around 2016, and for those years with actual scripts there was in addition just over a week's August Review marking spell in Manchester. I got to know and love the city well through this, if in defined places, these inevitably linked to where the hotel accommodation was for that year. It started in Rusholme at an independently owned hotel I over time got to know extremely well, including colleagues who also regularly stayed. That's a narrative in itself, so I'll confine myself to the locations, this one in Curry Mile – the areas and associations always based on where we drank and ate in the evenings, the marking taking place initially at the offices of the exam board, or in later years other hotels where we were booked with conference rooms for the work. The areas therefore changed so included Deansgate, Piccadilly, Palace Theatre locale and St Peter's Square. I've stayed twice in dives on the outskirts, Uriah Heap working at the one in Didsbury, and they don't retain the same celebratory memories. When you live rurally as I have done for over 40 years, a metropolitan environ is a vibrant change. A small core of friends and I would mainly socialise in the obvious ways already mentioned, but over the years I've engaged in/with events and activities specific to the city, not least the Manchester Jazz Festival, and at the theatre seeing a range from *Grease* (it was a whim and where the family sitting next to me sang every single song, to the letter) to Carol Churchill's *Skriker* staring an amazing Maxine Peake. I've seen Ron Sexsmith and then Gillian Welch play there, and in the early days I attended a poetry reading by James Tate as well as making a cheese sauce for Lemn Sissay – an anecdote I've ridden the back for years since. This is just a minor flavour, and it was the taste of a fine city. The more cosmopolitan experience was working with fellow senior examiners from across the country, and finding a core of lifelong friends. Each year, assistant examiners in your team were a kaleidoscope of skills required and not required for the job. Let's be clear – it's miserable pay for highly professional work. Most were always diligent, keen, attentive, and professional, especially in the days of face-to-face training where you developed informed, knowing relationships. When moderating their actual papers, you would see work in all its glory, *or* gory details. Digitally distant training has become the new norm, and despite the contrary statistical evidence – so I am told – it is not as effective as it was or needs to be, and with (ridiculously, in my view) only three terms' teaching experience now required to be such, compared with the three years when I started, membership of the opinionated Miserable Old Gits Affiliates has been duly allocated to me. My method of dealing with the impact of those worst offenders and the extra work they caused was to write gumshoe narratives about detecting and righting their wrongs, my persona Marker Mike hamming his best Chandler-esque dick scenarios to smooth out ruffled bed sheets or clear rats from behind the skirting boards.

Frog

The bucket was left out and upturned for weeks by the compost bin and was half full of stale rainwater. I decided to tip it out, and as I did, noticed at the last moment – slipping over the rim – the frog which had obviously been in there for a swim. But my noticing was actually a flashback of thinking I'd seen it floating within and then seeing again when poured out and falling to the ground. To be absolutely sure, I waited for the spreading pool of water to drain away in the dry soil, yet there was no frog to be seen. I assumed now it was a ghost of one, a snatched mental profile of the body, arms and legs all spread out as if reclining by a summer poolside expecting everything to be just fine, though in this instance no more than a phantom of such hopefulness.

When Olin was Stan

There was that new set of Stan pictures to confirm rather than tell any other stories, him striding and strutting with Bobbie Ann's mother on his arm out there peacock-walking after he'd strolled with mine, in another time, and there is a good chance (in the probability of him being a consummate Casanova) that there are more photos of kids pretending to play his over-sized guitar. It is increasingly clear how he liked to put his arms around women, or on his own: hands on hips and elbows out sideways to preen a tough-guy stance. There is a pair of pics of a visit to Ghost Town in 1973, those arms still embracing: here with two porcelain-modelled floozies in their ceramic smiles and one in a short red dress, no heart too hard to caress as long as you were there, sitting on that bench.

Lock

The lock went through the metal loop from the right, not the left as she did it – though I know it locked in both positions – and while this wasn't the only difference that did not matter, there was more than allegory in this varying way we secured what was behind those doors. It was the same with our eating diverse meals at our differing times, or how each night as she would go to sleep, I would go on the following day. And though we rose at similar moments, it would be like this for the rest of our lives, each of us heading for the equivalent place by alternative routes.

Holiday Reading at Port Launay

Interrupting Ellroy, I sensed and then found the decomposing body of a swan floating ass-up at a hook in the river, definitely the stench speaking out between the lines to stop my reading: flies laying eggs on darkened feathers where he was sans mate but where French kisses once hen-pecked him to love (*hickeys sure as shit*, James echoed from what I had managed to take in that far) recalling this pair the last time I had read here. At first, I'd contemplated a human corpse from its distant floating shadow – some other upstream terrorism – but it made little sense, knowing, to feel worse then. Many relationships reach an end yet this one pained more than any story somehow.

My Wild Dog

I had my first pet dog at my first home in Norfolk, Nebraska when I was probably 9 years old. He was a collie-mongrel called Pepper and was wild – but not quite the wolf chained up under Uncle Clyde's porch in Niobrara where you had to collect water from a pump and shit in an outhouse the local boys would push over whilst you were performing (it happened to Aunt Jenny, but perhaps only that one time). It was obvious he was getting mean the day I got home from school and found my tamed red squirrel torn to pieces. So, it was time to let Pepper go, an animal doing unto another like that acknowledged as unacceptable even in my childlike take on the rights and wrongs of things – and a double tragedy in such a concurrent loss. It was about a week later when the farmer who had responded to our give-away advertisement called around personally to return Pepper's leash and, no doubt trying to be kind and positive, said *his* dog now was chasing sheep for fun and running free and living a life that eviscerating my other pet was also just the manifestation of what should be.

Chopping Wood

I'd hit myself with the axe twice in the space of a few weeks – the first a glancing blow off the shin (with a blunt blade to thank for that) and the second a follow-through onto the bridge of my left foot, but neither thankfully a gash or a slice or worse an amputation which would have been disastrous – therefore I may have to give up chopping wood, or learn to be a surgeon should the former good decision not prevail, because I don't believe this favourable fortune or being crap in my swing was a meaningless forewarning.

Leaving the Job

Having taught English for 30 years, I took early retirement from teaching for personal reasons in 2010. I've said since with gest, but some seriousness too, that it was also a good time to go: before I killed someone or the job killed me. Having had half a career of absolute bliss in a creative, independent and vibrant world of education, the latter years were increasingly controlled by external interference from political philistinism and a culture of target-setting with performance judgements based on this. It became a withering experience. Teaching colleagues were always wonderful, especially the English teams, and students even more so. It is such a privilege to work a lifetime with young people – this including 13 years as a Youth Worker at my school, helping to run a Monday night social and sports club. The early years of my career were full of hope and fun and freedom, this with inspirational leadership for my subject specialism as well as from certain individuals within school. The latter years chipped away at my joy, control from frauds and dumb idealogues taking over. I should focus here on the good times and especially people, but they know who they are and have had my thanks and celebrations when it mattered – much of this in my retirement leaving speech which, I am told, was interminably long. I cannot deny this, and have always felt genuine sympathy for those who had to stand for the duration when all the seats were taken in our staffroom. The bad times and especially linked people were, as I've said, mainly political idiots – especially Education Secretaries – and in their detrimental impact on me as a person and a professional, I am unforgiving. But for those who were teachers with influence and who took on the maxims, mantras and mechanisms of such external interferences – and through which they could then be critical of fellow colleagues – I reserve the most disdain. There was one who once offered support to me by email and through the office of a local advisory position. It was 'help' with analysing my English department's Key Stage 3 SATs results at the time, tests I detested and did not value one iota since their inception. I immediately sent an email to my Headmaster letting him know what I thought of such an offer of assistance, explaining in my anger that 'I'd rather poke out my eyes with a javelin'. As has happened with so many others since the regular use of technological communication, and as will happen again and again, I in fact responded directly back to the advisor, using *Reply* by error, not individually emailing my Headmaster. I did regret the mistake and informed the person of this, apologising, not wanting to be that unprofessional in such a candid, brutal response. And while I don't regret now my better judgement in saying sorry then, I don't today regret my brute honesty. It will seem like brooding, but in ten years of being retired from the day to day, you have time to recall, and the subsequent 'advisory' influence from this person when I was still working did much to make me weary because of its critical, manipulative payback, though that person may have felt they had a point to prove. While to this day I do think the 'javelin in the eyes' metaphor was apt and dramatically so, I am aware it does poke a hole in what has always been my adamant stance on the requisites for the formal, *polite* but firm letter of complaint – or in this case, an unintentional email.

On my leaving, this plaque was placed at the entrance to English teaching rooms by my lovely team. An 'alternative' version was put in the English office where, from memory, one of its three attributes was 'tosser'...!

Moles Again

The moles and I reached an agreement over the many years and I've probably only killed one or two in a long while, though not for want of trying: I have lost many of the necessary skills. There is a solo molehill near the door of the bigger shed, but it is close enough to a wild part of the garden so I've left it there – not even bothering to level it out for the aesthetics of this situation, and being content now for it to live anywhere nearby. The other is just into and on the front lawn, the two perpendicular silvery arms of the set trap not yet splayed to let me know *that* one is definitely gone. A while back I'd called in an expert, my stalking days no longer the success of my past expertise, but he'd little luck too and I found the same snare online he used at a fraction of his cost. How so much has changed though not the other cruelties and deeper darknesses and outbreaks of human misery; the bigger decisions to make in being humane. And like all change, this catch-up and summation is now in prose.

Three Young Boys Camping Briefly in the Taunus Mountains near Frankfurt

I would have been 11 or 12, my friend the same age, and his brother made up our trio, aged 14: the older sister was not on that day a part of our tempting adventure to come. We were all then so young to be journeying into any darkness, let alone the one which would obviously expose the fragile grip on a situation our naïve experience and imagination would so easily dismantle. That we were let out on our own this late afternoon, for a known trip with a tent and, I presume, a few other essentials to make our way to the Taunus mountains for a camp-out, is tantamount to abject parental incompetence and/or indifference. Not likely to have been too far away, we walked and searched and climbed and pitched and settled in for the night, but it wasn't long before bears and wolves and other evils had us packing away like a comically accelerated film and arriving back much later in an unknown town, exhausted, starting to put the tent up on an unknown someone's front lawn. The polizei found us, obviously alerted by the incredulous owners of the home whose garden we attempted to appropriate, and after awkward communications at the police station, fuelled by language difficulties and our increasing anxieties, we were driven back to my friend's house, no siren announcing our return. The night before I'd encountered another forest to touch upon and then be scared away, a different siren raising its silent tempting alarm.

Giving Up

I started smoking cigarettes aged 11 outside the Yellow Building opposite the entrance to Karlsruhe AHS. This is where all the 'cool-heads' would hang out and there was an element of defiance in smoking so openly which was technically against the rules though we weren't on school property. We didn't hide our collective rule-breaking and that was our *cool* disobedience. At my peak in later teens in England I did smoke 60 a day, a combination of Consulate menthols and unfiltered cigarettes, perhaps Woodbines, but usually others, and very occasional Russian Sobranies. Aged 19, I stopped. Cold turkey. I may have succumbed to one or two since that time, but genuinely no more than this. It was the same with LSD. I'd always had good experiences with this, a combination of unsullied product, good luck and my own mental health stability. I suspect luck is/was the key factor; also never being assailed by external madnesses, apart from that plastic policeman. So, when I couldn't control the time of when to come down from a trip, I simply stopped altogether. At the risk of sounding triumphal in my decisiveness, I've never managed the same tough management over snacking and unhealthy eating in general, or drinking alcohol. That said, as I get older, moderation as an instinct has replaced abstinence, so that is some kind of progress, and it won't be the tobacco, acid or bourbon that does me in, but Cheetos and chili dogs instead.

Searching but Not Finding My Name at *ResearchGate*

this is not me reaping the benefits / this is not my intelligent route to business / this is not intraplaque haemorrhage for me by me about me / this is not a lifetime wool survival and this is not a new method for monitoring a 2-megawatt high voltage test load but it could be the critical plaque wall stress in human atherosclerotic plaque if I had written / but this is not me in the progeny birth weights intelligence platform and this is not even strategic interaction / and this is not committing and detecting fraudulent multispecies forests / this is not never was never will be my yield regulation for multi-aged care provision / this is not me me me me / this is testing plasma pools but not me / this is this / this is not markers for vitral contamination unless a burroughs but not me / this is an unconventional approach but not a quantifying effect of not being not me

Aasta May, Mom

Sharing a love of words, I should have shared more time valuing the long and short of it all – vowels beautifully balanced across a name, that balancing in saying I could leave when I might have remained, then living so far away it would always be down to language keeping us close, expressions of closeness never lost when stretched across years and miles. Reading between the lines of that stretch was another act of poise, but there were no shortcomings then or now, and these words will not be chimed to be more than sound. Not yet. Her words to me were always honest and true – poetry and letters to a son in England, a blend of our roots and a selfless faith in the future, showing me how to keep it simple: always Mom, not Mum.

Raking Leaves

I would be in the garden raking autumn leaves into piles ready for composting and then pause for a moment to look up at the sky where the blue or grey – depending upon the whim of that day – asked me to stop and consider. There are ways to rake leaves: one is simply an expense of energy making random mounds; another is to walk up and down forming two parallel lines that are then collected into neat and even piles. Whatever the design, more will be falling in the days that followed. I'd start by dressing warm but the heat would soon build and I'd need to remove clothing or slow down. The grass would reveal its expanse of green and summer gone, but I knew there was much more work to be done.

High Tide at Sidmouth Where We'd Always Go

Lying flat out on the pavement, perhaps dying, she would be inevitable in a town full of old people. But what should I have made of the whole three-foot cod floundered high on the promenade's hard – a lone seagull chaperoning rather than on the gorge – or the tern turned belly-up on the beach at the tide-mark's highest edge (equally as dead as that fish) because once I was home later in the day, these high tides would divine irrelevance in the wider scheme of personal preoccupations?

NFL in the UK

The NFL came to British TV screens in 1982 via Channel 4 and I discovered my national game through this British presentation – I'd had stateside school and local park playing, but that had been it. I began videoing games and watched every Superbowl shown, only missing one year when the power failed. In those early days I introduced the sport to my Monday night school youth club when students had become big fans too. I also knew how to throw the ball so assumed the quarterback role *naturally* for that reason, running plays in the school hall. The first NFL game I ever saw was The American Bowl with my dad at Wembley Stadium in 1986. He must have been living and working in Beaconsfield or Belgium at the time: one of the two Bs, but I can't recall which. The game was between then Superbowl champions Chicago Bears and the Dallas Cowboys, the Bears fielding quarterback Jim McMahon, running-back Walter Payton, and the appliance that was William 'The Refrigerator' Perry. Since the NFL came to London for its regular season games, I've gone to as many as I could (afford), and the greatest outings were with my girls, especially both together, and the best of this is when we saw the Oakland Raiders – designated home team and Karis' favourite – play the Miami Dolphins in 2014. Ana and I had been to the States that summer and so we bought our Raiders gear for the game, and they added to this for the day.

In-Laws at Ninety

When I talked to her it was to the hard flat of a wall. My comment on Bill writing of standing atop a box and seeing the whole of Iowa was stopped entirely at its inner stone so she also didn't hear when I added how, like Bryson, I still loved it here, and family. But *he* listened and received it all, welcomed words with new understanding, though I knew it would soon enough dissolve. He had asked the same things so many times already, but at least was making enquiries – each instant full, for a while. If making it, he was two months shy of them both being ninety. Now under his breath so she could not pick this one up in life's love of an ironic moment, he said he'd ask to go into hospital as they could no longer cope at their age – and this was heard loud and clear, the decision shared in the moment of our leaving.

Waiting at Thornaby for the Train

I didn't see waterfowl flying when I was either coming or going, but I heard about them at my dear friend Andy's funeral. All I saw while waiting were the backs of buildings and two lines either side of the station. In Yarm where he was going to be buried, talk was of travellers who would soon arrive for the Fair and of shops that would or would not be open for that time. I wanted to see and sit at the deli where he had his morning coffees and the chocolate croissant which melted in summer's heat, but it had already closed early for the coming week, and my pilgrimage was stopped by expectant fear. He'd been wild – wildly in his head and then when this took over: flights of the unexpected and dangerously funny, but he was always good – the palliative he shared despite his growing noir. Andy wasn't scared and had planned the poems read, *Wild Geese* soaring above what the preacher said.

Marvin Hugh

My father was the son of Grandma Fergy and this is why we had to occasionally visit her shack in Niobrara where he was born, bring water inside from a pump that seemed miles away, brave an outhouse, and beware a probable wolf nearby. There was enduring his sense of humour when being breathed on after he'd eaten Limburger cheese with its Brevibacterium linens (yes, the same that causes body and foot odour) purchased locally on the drive to hers. We'd also eat authentic and wonderful frankfurters bought at an isolated farm-butchers on that same journey there and where you didn't see any chainsaws lying around. These were not intentionally bad experiences – apart from the 'comic' cheese-breath, and excepting the wieners – though they were a challenge. I have some positive memories of Niobrara: crushed-ice root beer from a drive-in near the shack; searching through and getting occasional paperbacks and other paraphernalia from one of those classic Aladdin Cave small-town drug stores; being taken to the local bar run by two brothers, and visiting with other family who I never got to know that well – being accidently burnt on the cheek by her cigarette when sitting in the lap of an older pretty cousin while watching a movie at the downtown picture house. But growing up in all the other places had tough, often mean times, and these paint a personal picture that dominates memory. Once beyond these, aged 16 and living in England, my father did support me financially in the early years of this escape, making it possible. And further beyond, forging my way, I'd like to think there was a respect, not that it was ever directly conveyed. Later gestures were the only touchstone I had for a sense of change, some larger than others. There was the holiday to the States with my family: an expensive rental in Ashland paid for, and the use of his van during our West

Coast trip to San Francisco and its sights: Monterey for Steinbeck and where Jimi played, Santa Cruz to ride The Giant Dipper, and Carmel with its 17-mile drive (though using that van for a month without our 'promised' insurance-cover still makes me shudder, working out its absence years later). And that financial investment in me/us cost him dearly – I think my working hard on a farm and at studying and then three jobs for much of my life made me less tolerant of anyone so much less prudent. I'd say we were at our closest and most relaxed on the phone over the latter years. He'd always want to talk football, NFL and the English game – like me, still a fan of Ipswich Town FC – but having an extraordinary memory for matches watched and especially 'soccer': he could recall things in the games here I couldn't remember or just didn't know. This is when he was at his most engaged and empathetic, something we could share, though I can't romanticise things beyond their reality, like I won't Stan's infidelities. And unlike Marvin Hugh, Stan was never a part of the family, didn't know I had one and never held his grandchildren or show any kind of care, good or bad, when he could and might have tried. So, I do need to and will be relative and not rose-tinted in my memory; always try to be the father *I* want to be.

Talent, Oregon, 2010: I lost again

Finding Tom

When I wasn't looking, Tom suddenly appeared. He is my older brother by four years and was born to our mother Aasta May when so many miles away from her family and home. Tom was adopted in April 1950, four or six weeks after his birth, and it took 65 years for me to learn about any of this. Since acquiring such knowledge, I have layered much of its warm and welcome certainty with surmise and deduction, each strand of imagining attached to increasing feelings of sadness for mom giving up a son I am sure she wanted to love. I can never know for sure why she journeyed the nearly 500 miles from Omaha to Denver to give birth, but researching reveals that at the Florence Crittenton Home where Tom was born, the rule was he, like all new babies, would be given up for adoption – mothers there for that very reason and with the dreadful motivation usually being concealment of a family's embarrassment and shame. I might assume our mother asked the Lutheran Social Services to handle that adoption – one of three commonest 'agency' choices – but I can never know for sure why she christened my brother *Michael*, though I can also assume this was her reason for giving the same meaningful name to me.

Words

In the three-phrasal chorus to the Bee Gees song *Words*, Barry Gibb sings 'It's only words' which is rather dismissive, but he salvages an awareness of their dynamism within language usage by the subsequent intoning 'and words are all I have' which is, of course, the core attribute of our being human. The third phrase moves on to romanticism, and that's another trajectory. In explaining the meaning behind this song, Robin Gibb keeps it simple: 'words can make you happy or words can make you sad', but I am here more interested in my American/English journey with them. I have been prompted to this exploration by listening to the eponymous album by Jackson C. Frank, he singing *Kimbie* with its line 'Let your hair hang down / And your bangs all curl around'. On arriving in England in 1967, I had a set of expectations, the first that we spoke the same language – this soon to be regularly challenged, as was a notion that most business men wore pin-striped suits with bowler hats while everyone else was mainly dressed in Afghan coats and other multi-coloured accompaniments. In language term differences I did know there would be a few 'foreign' words encountered: before moving to England, I was in Germany and remember a group of us reading a pop magazine at the Yellow Building, coming across an article on the Beatles and Carnaby Street (thus some of the dress expectations) and discovered the word 'knarked' used in its storyline. It's hard to convey how as Americans we were so excited about this exotic verb, and it entered our own vocabulary for at least a couple of weeks. In reality, once in England the words that became regular new discoveries were all nouns, and their contraries hardly prevented communication: bangs/fringe; trunk/boot; fender/bumper; hood/bonnet (and how automotive as well as twee many English alternatives often were); faucet /tap,

153

and so on. There were obviously slang differences, and Americanisms along this line have over time defaulted in the UK to those transatlantic roots, though 'far-out' as an expression of wonder does seem to be an anachronism peculiar to my instinctive exclamations. When a teacher, I had to see the Headmaster at my school at least three times for corrective chastisement of my language practice in the classroom: the use of *bloody*, a word I'd picked up living here and simply an adjectival intensifier rather than a 'profane' one; the use of *bum* – a comic semantical difference in application – my using to characterise someone being lazy, and probably whimsically so (its derivation linked derogatorily to 'hobo', and never my intention and simply about personal motivation), and the use of *jesus christ*, another automatic expression as an American, for me an exasperation, and certainly not the blaspheme about which a parent had complained. More broadly I know I continually use American words/phrases in my writing, regularly prefer the connective *and* over more complex sentence structures, and when swearing prefer *ass* to *arse*, though I do think this latter a 'sweeter' British name-call, like *knob* and *bell-end* and similar. I have a close friend today whose language proclivities are as individually acquired and applied as mine are, his being the (occasional rather than pervasive) Germanic, so *schadenfreude, weltanschauung, zeitgeist,* and recently in an email, *wohlgemut.* As they say: jeder für sich.

Ants and the Poetry Stones at Ottery

The ants would appear to be no lovers of verse, though if having a proclivity, they'd perhaps be silly for a rhyme like *worse* because they love the crack, excusing the pun too as I mean the cracks between granite stones that really came all the way from China to carry Samuel Taylor Coleridge's words. Walking that day along the entire run of *Kubla Khan,* I saw the skateboard grazes, mud traces of cycle tyre treads, and footprints using *Ancestral voices* and other phrases as stepping stones from path to grass at the Land of Canaan where this poem lay. Ottery's Poetry Stones – the longest laid alfresco poem in the land, though measureless to a man from 'The Guinness Book of Records' because unique: an obtuse decree – could not deter the ants whose triangles of mounded dirt rose between the gaps that allow this curve of Samuel's words to make their igneous way along the tarmac track. It was a while back that someone observed how within these carved meandering lines a connective or preposition was incorrectly placed, though meaning is clearly not compromised as passers-by follow unencumbered from error when girdled round, reading for pleasure at their own casual pace. I imagine Coleridge's preference for the irreverence of free-spirited scuffs: accidents instead of pedants.

Murray Dance Instructor

Being a Murray Dance Instructor in the 50s and 60s was quite likely a cool thing to do: post-war / post-depression, and life on the rise, relatively speaking, with a part-time job to help the ascent. He will have fancied himself, possessing a few moves – they might well have been called *skills* – and an ambition to take the many 'ladies' on their individual twirls. I'd imagine his male friends referred to him as Stan the Man, being in a knowing gender groove, but also guess he'd have put a more sophisticated tag out there like Olin, the Swede of Swing. This is one way to bait the hook. My mother was caught, and those other women, including the ones who became wives and/or moms: the children to either shimmy along or get dropped like a failed lift on the way. *Arthur Murray Taught me Dancing in a Hurry* may well have been his mantra of the time, personal tuition so much more expedient than mail-order footprint diagrams. We know the appeal still – just think of that *Strictly* history. I've always thought of myself as much more than a dad-dancer (but forever a father), moves honed through a lifelong love of music and bourbon: definitely not an Art of the Heartbreaker played on that guitar of his which was less faithful, ironically, than one shaped like a valentine.

The Importance of Music in 1971: 3

Conway Twitty released two albums in 1971, *How Much More Can She Stand* and *I Wonder What She'll Think About Me Leaving,* but I wasn't really the hardened fan yet, more into peace and love and West Coast harmonies – psychedelia too – rather than the mature man's angst about who was contemplating desertion from a strained relationship, and especially as I was only starting my great love affair. Incipient C&W sensibilities were better served by another '71 release with leanings toward this genre – Micky Newbury's *Frisco Mabel Joy* and the track 'An American Trilogy' made famous by Elvis Presley a year later. Therefore, my norm preferences were served further by Joni Mitchell's sublime *Blue*, Carol King's astonishing *Tapestry*, and James Taylor's *Mud Slide Slim and the Blue Horizon.* Heavier sounds were delivered by Curved Air's *Second Album* and Yes' *Fragile,* among others. When David Bowie released *Hunky Dorey*, I heard the spaceman's re-entry with ideas from beyond. My wild card choice in this brief account (which didn't have such a category as I began writing it) would be The Guess Who's *So Long Ballantyne.* Just a year before, *American Woman* suggested a different musical trajectory, but here was honkey tonk blues, comic turns about 'fiddlin', beautiful piano balladry with light orchestra in *Sour Suite*, retro rock'n'roll, and consummate jazz with further orchestration in the songwriting and performance of *Goin' a Little Crazy.* A great year in my musical life.

Recliners

I had put both recliners out on the patio, side by side, just in case. I knew the weather would continue its fortuity, and it wasn't as if this was the dance we could never have or a jaunt through a forest and along the seashore for miles – not even a meal at the same time – but there was a chance that if the sun decided to shine again at that backend of a very long winter, we might have grabbed our moment together. Spring had been in the air that day and it was natural to think like this as well as all the clearing away, throwing out and planning what could be done next, all being well, even though much would stay the same and there was some comfort in this and how it would best the sign of any decline.

Alma and Mr D

Jules Drohlich – or Mr D as we all knew him – was Aunt Alma's husband and the only person in our family who was wealthy, or so it seemed to me. This was probably as a relative reality when, for example, on childhood birthdays and Christmases I'd be given ten individual one-dollar bills in a fat plain white envelope. There were other, surer signals: he always had a wad of notes neatly folded into a silver clip in his trouser pocket, and they weren't singles; he was the manager at one of the larger Omaha hotels – a seeming figurehead there where we occasionally dined and he was clearly in charge, and the fact other regular gifts when visiting their apartment were always little collections of hotel paraphernalia (not that I was aware of these origins then) so pens and further stationery items, fingernail clippers, insignia pins and all kinds of other shiny objects that were completely useless to a child but all the more precious for this otherworldliness. Mr D only had two modes of dress: a black suit which he wore with white shirt and black tie, and white boxer underpants with a white sleeveless vest he'd wear sitting next to a fan in that hot summer Omaha apartment which seemed exotic because it wasn't a house and had long linear rooms with at least a couple of doors which could open onto a hallway. Aunt Alma was my mother's older sister and the boss, a Director of Nurses who also served as a young nurse in New Guinea during the second world war. She was fierce and fiercely independent, but always kind to me – indeed, she looked after Melanie and me in so many ways when I was a child in those early days of living in Omaha and Elk Horn. She was the one who had to drive me back to Oakland, having already taken me to Omaha airport with my useless family passport, and it won't be the first time she was scathing about my father and his organising of our family life. I think

159

she 'helped out' my mother's life more than I ever experienced or subsequently knew, perhaps making that tough trip to Denver with her in 1950. She took a supportive interest in mine, especially when I moved to England, eventually studying at Oxford and becoming a teacher. She valued my academic achievements and my writing. I once wrote a poem for her with the opening lines *The filter wears a crimson kiss;/ mug-brims too sport / lipstick crescents with coffee stains. / She is tattooing things with codes, / a few decals announcing her like billboards.* Fond references to visual memories, but the poem's next lines *From sentences sanded through larynx bobs / her phrases growl out to press into my ears* – caused her some hurt, thinking I was being critical, but I assured her of their equally fond foundations and think she understood. My instinct in not recalling with Alma that time I took her to the Oxford Playhouse was no doubt correct on this aspect: knowing we were going to see Beckett's *Endgame*, she read my copy of the play in preparation. During the performance, sitting centrally and near the stage, when Clov walked around with a certain item in his hands, Alma turned to me and said in her softest foghorn voice 'Now we know what a gaff is Mike' for everyone else to hear. I was youngish, probably too precious about being at the theatre, was embarrassed by her brash American voice, and I do regret being annoyed. Go on Clov, you can hit me now with your gaff because of mine: I deserve it.

Our Days Out

There's a line from Les Dawson that I'll hazard a guess could have us all laughing on our annual day out when examining in Manchester, not that I'll repeat it here or that we needed another's humour to keep us amused: our two regular colleague guides on one day could be George and Lennie *leading* the way – that's a joke – or on another, Gogo climbing the hill for his dear friend Didi to have a look onwards and try and find where we were going. Friendships extend to unknown places, and the unexpected, where we all found so much more each year and on those excursions. We had to travel all this way to see one another, put the world to rights for that year, when at work and homes from across the country we were time's strangers – our days and days in the different out-of-focus of routine. But when *out*, it might be getting lost yet again along that landmark Manchester Ship Canal towards Salford, or ending up in the city's sewers when those underground tours were allowed and where the gag was on us as it was so much fun, camaraderie in the dark and lavatorial, laughter however we made it, or as Les might have told it to us at our one trip to Blackpool and where we shared such spontaneous joy walking and reading the Comedy Carpet at the Tower Festival Headland.

A Misunderstanding

When my two second-hand copies of Gerald Locklin books arrived in the post it proved to be a slightly confused day. There was his spoof *the case of the missing blue volkswagon* as well as *Candy Bars*, a collection of short stories. I was looking at the latter when I first came across pencil and pen handwritten notes on the title story, not his, but then further in were two actual photographs of Gerald which I think must have been personal snaps because on the back they were process-stamped with *Barbra Locklin* and I didn't really know what all of this meant, yet I was shouting out how great it all was when Val said 'that's not very good' and I asked her why and she said, I think humorously, 'someone leaving their rubbish behind' so I told her it was a brilliant thing to find, and then next I was shouting '£300!' and she said 'now *that's* brilliant' but I'd moved on and had opened up my car tax bill which wasn't even a Volkswagen or a Dodge like his father used to have, or the Pontiac he had driven Gerald in down to Henner and Bennet's bar and grill – but my car was also blue and on good days I could put the top down.

Her Ghost Voice

It is that time and I hear her call but it is a ghost haunting ahead of its moment, a voice that urges and implores before the need is even more. Each night I will pause and listen and hear: sometimes it is the shout that pierces, or it is just shadow, the dark echo from before rounded out to an almost sound as if real. And I respond. I rise and wait and listen and hear the eventual silence like some blessing; and blessed, I take my place back in the queue to await the sound of her actual call, whenever there is the impulse of her need. And as the time comes for her sharp appeal, it is a call I am so well-rehearsed to heed.

Immigrant Irony

There was that boorish sideswipe again, some little Englander telling me Americans do not understand irony just before claiming *I want my country back.* I want mine back too, *this* one I've lived in since 1967; a permanent resident – that important legal acquisition in these days of sending back – from 1976, a mirror reflected year with my having left family behind, also those small-town thugs who wanted me dead and other redneck retributions for a difference that didn't seem to matter walking home unafraid in Suffolk's midnight darkened roads, long hair no longer dodging the beer cans or a tree branch ripped from a neighbour's yard to take a different kind of swing. These obvious violences didn't run to blood in *our* rivers, but hatred has always been with us, though then tolerances defined a whole instead of today's long line of fear pasted on billboards to create rather than cover every growing crack: so listen to me, any little mad Englander out there, I want *my* country back.

Along the River Otter

My friends called around as arranged to take their dogs for a walk along the River Otter: the old collie on a lead, not to stop it running away, but to keep it moving; the middle one a normal dog, and then the third that was taking speed. They told me about their reading that day, relaxing, and we drove and parked at a place where there were scattered cut tree trunks and other wood to take away for free, ready for winter when it came, months along, but they were preparing. We headed down to the river across fields in the blazing sun. Both threw balls, and the dog on amphetamines collected and came back each time more eager than before, shaking water from the stream on our summery bare legs to cool us in that heated July tolerance. When I was home later and reading Larry Brown's short story *92 Days* – where it was also hot – I was drinking too, and his world of pick-ups and beer and writing seemed so true in what it was obviously missing. Like him, I wanted to know where this one was going to go, if anywhere, as once the wood was piled and that dog sedated by nightfall, all there'd be were the following days with nothing new for anyone to desire.

Fall like the French Off a Ladder

I was trying to be French, l' élagage, or more precisely, existential – you know, Satre and all – but it was only during the fall from a ladder and waiting to land on my back when I wondered what would be the essence of such a breakage. This was a lifetime's third major drop: once taking out a whole rhododendron on landing; a second, wrenching my arm when lessening the descent, and that day's complete backwards arc to hit the ground in my own thunder. But I couldn't then speak French if trying, the tip still there but a teeth-drawn line on the tongue where a full bite might have been, as precarious as that fourth rung.

Wheels

Out for a walk up the lane one morning, I moved over for the tractor and huge trailer to pass, its beautiful sweet rot of silage wafting me back over forty years and especially to that Christmas morning feeding livestock and the thrill of her with me in the cab, the other buzz as we slid at speed down the dewy hill – differential beyond control and a ton of pungent maize thrusting from behind with wheels locked so that even surviving intact couldn't take the dark rush of that movement away. So, in current times we have still sought out the existential, though on other wheels, driving the blue hot rod well over 100 on that last bend up the by-pass before turning off towards home. It's all OK as long as these wheels don't fall off, and for obvious but also different reasons we can't rely on our legs for moving out into the faster lane, another weight pushing from behind.

If

If I am gone, I would be concerned retrospectively, so-to-speak, on whether she will be able to find things like the obvious of important documents, pension, entitlements, various commitments, Will, and renewals; the passwords for every online account of what we have become; then the chargers for electricals like vacuums – upright and hand-held – power tools (not that she would use and not that she couldn't), phones, tablets; and speaking of tablets, there's the medicines (those that work/ed); the bank account details, savings in her name, accident insurance that could be so ironic – me and ladders; the obvious personal things like photo albums, photos on the computer, letters, old family videos; and the record collection, and all those books that will need sorting – mine are in two places, archives of ambition; the so many poems I have written about her and us, not sharing directly but direct, years of recording and reflecting and about being as one, about the slowed journey together; or if she found this first written here and now for fulfilling, so struck by its pragmatism and so compelled to find all the others that are not so practical.

My Daughter's Music

I lost myself was a chorus echoing from the crowd as the concert ended and I wonder when it hit Ana, that plaintive note amidst the reverie where nostalgia is both joy and pain, remembering how years have gone – and, of course, my refrains have played out so many times before, lost or found. For her it could have been at the metaphor of an *Airbag*, its sudden jolt on how those dreams are lost even if in what was found. And did we think it all *OK* together in the 'dining' room, my discovery of a new psychedelia in the *Android*, her having already travelled? On this night, *karma* is resolution rather than retribution, an evening out of lives late into the dark. Music always held us tight and she'd have missed being there, and me missing her here.

Gods of Rock

I never named our 'teachers' band so pompously, and I'm sure it was meant to be fondly ironic from whoever did. And whatever we were in status and quality, it was only ever annual – playing at our school's summer Festival on the Field (renaming Sports Day more inclusively) in the actually non-competitive Battle of the Bands and where all groups performed on an unhitched lorry trailer from a local haulier. The students were regularly outstanding – with many going on to record and perform in their various later professional formations. I played bass on the GOR covers of Bon Jovi, Queen, Free, Tom Petty and other classic rock names, and never wore a wig.

Aeolian Harp

Living now in the town of Samuel Taylor Coleridge's birth
I have grown to know him quite well. Much of this is
because of seeing him when we're both out walking the
same locality, crossing the bridge over the River Otter and
watching the egret he did all those years ago, or hearing him
read his poem *Kubla Khan* aloud as I stroll alongside at the
Land of Canaan. Much of my knowing is obviously from
reading his poetry, but also the letters and philosophical
musings, this latter as intense as comparing and contrasting
the merits of coal and wood fires, or his spiritual
rollercoaster rides. Being involved in local fundraising for
a memorial statue has added to the deep overall awareness,
my never, ironically, the world's biggest enthusiast for such
bronze or stone effigies, but wholly accepting the
conventional, traditional need. If it had been my choice
there would be a commemorative Aeolian harp, giant-sized,
like the one in Negrar over six meters high, or another at
the Exploratorium in San Francisco. It is difficult to
imagine where it could be placed here, as even at the fields
by the river it would serenade people in houses on the slight
hillside above, who, if liking Coleridge at all, might
otherwise prefer a sculpture's silence. Wherever this could
have been placed it would to my mind play the essence of
him and that one time he coalesced with everything
personally meaningful, *A light in sound, a sound-like power
in light, / Rhythm in all thought, and joyance everywhere* –
which I would remind him again and again in future
passings.

When they offered to Tarmac the Driveway for Free, I Declined

From over the years: that's my cars' oil stains there and there and there / that's where I drove in and out to work for thirty years / that's her initials, somewhere / that's where I made it home drunk, swearing and banging on the window / that dip has been worn down by walking to and from the garden / that's where I parked the truck with all our furniture and us in 1980 / that's next to the gate which used to be hung at the entrance / that's where I painted the crap hood of the charcoal coloured car and made it worse / that's our grey and gravel and grooves / that's where I've backed in as much as I've driven out / that's the indentations drawn by wheels for over forty years / that's where we brought her home / that's the area she was made to clean it up / that's where we'll continue to come and go as it always has been – so I'll leave the drive as it is, thank you.

Lockdown, Empty Suitcase and an Aeolian Washburn

Unable to travel, I wouldn't be making that annual trip to Manchester – thirty-five years and never missed – so moving in a bedroom's tight space to put the empty suitcase away, I knocked it over to fall and brush across the Washburn on its stand, open-tuned to E, and though not quite a beginning to a blues, it was a perfect chord playing how many good things remained.

Should I Go or Should I Stay?

In my working life, I've considered leaving the teaching job on a number of occasions. The first was early on when there were financial struggles – though I make no claim to experiencing real poverty, and fully stress the significant relativity of things I'll recall. I did always graft extremely hard and know my salary in those early years was not good and didn't compare favourably with other similar professions. Indeed, so strong were my feelings I once reported the *Daily Express* newspaper to the Press Council for inaccurate reporting on teacher pay claims at the time. Obviously, as a Tory/right-wing rag, it's views on teachers were full of inaccuracies and provocative lies. This turned out to be a lengthy set of communications between myself, the paper's editor and the Press Council. However, and obviously again, I lost my complaint, though the PC's published commentary acknowledged elements of the paper's misrepresentation, excusing this as opinion. My first near commitment to leaving was when considering the photocopier technician's visits to my school: he arrived in a company car, didn't seem to have a particularly challenging job, and earned a better salary than me. One Sunday working as usual preparing teaching resources, I stopped what I was doing and typed a letter of application for a position at Rank Xerox. It was a letter of genuine anger and desperation, though I later decided not to send. As I've said, struggles were relative: I had a regular income; I was living in council rented accommodation, yet secured; there were luxuries I couldn't afford, but we didn't go without, and while we couldn't take holidays abroad – going instead, for example, to a Camelford Cornwall holiday camp where the town a few years earlier had a major water-poisoning incident and thus prices were still considerably lower than anywhere else – we did enjoy regular local caravan site holidays as a family, still cheapish and not with the stigma of threats to health. There were other occasions when I thought, because of an uncertainty, I would have to leave work to be instead at home. For one I started writing 'Occupation' list poems, choosing all the obvious professions and providing apt illustrations which I thought could be framed and have a potential global market as attractive and focused 'what can I get?' presents for family/friends – *everyone has a job/profession* ironic logic from me – and though I couldn't even get local businesses interested (my *MAS* experience all over again), these did much later appear as my *Professions* poetry chapbook collection. For another, when I desperately thought I needed some alternative means of earning, once more from home, I began writing C&W lyrics to sell to the stars – though Conway Twitty was no longer with us, having passed in '93. I initially wrote what I thought an archetypal lyric of considerable charm and appeal titled *My Ol' Waist Size* with wry observations on getting older and facing up to the physical changes, this employing a classic use of clever-clogs if banal rhyming couplets. I never had to commit to either desperate venture, and sadly the potential C&W musical paean is currently misplaced.

First Car

The illusion is in my pose: 'racing' sunglasses and the way the car's whole front body hinged to open forwards and look impressive, as if to reveal something significant, though those in the know will immediately work out it definitely isn't a hot rod. If it was a Vitesse, that'd be different, but it is instead a sedate Triumph Herald with a 1296 cc engine. This was a most welcome wedding present in 1976 from my new in-laws, and it moved me and Val first to Ibstone and then later to Devon, leaving its oil and memories on the driveway there. I did *hot-rodise* it a little in the early 80s, putting on a small steering wheel – the fad then – which did make it fun to drive with its short arc for moving left or right, and after installing a cassette player, I included additional speakers: two large ones from an old Amstrad where I trimmed the wood casings so each would fit under the front seats. As with cars of that time, it began to rust quickly, and despite my efforts to keep the exterior pretty with the promises of all those lying rust-proofing paints, the corrosion advanced to the front outriggers and it collapsed. The Triumph was replaced by a sleek-looking Citroen CX with its sense of elegance as well as glide-like adjustable suspension. It was painted a wonderful metallic light green but I hadn't spotted the bodywork filler which exposed its fakery soon enough. I won't narrate that night when, blind drunk with a friend, we ISOPONed it – and then the next morning's sobering-up discovery of this catastrophic mess.

Poser with Triumph Herald

Some Diurnal Aural Awe

This is the playful but also satirical name of my music blog with its inverted take on the American catch-all expression *awesome*, me preferring *far out* as both an instinctive vocal veneration and hippie-era time dating. My love of music was imbued through whatever was played on the radio as I was growing up, therefore Perry Como, Andy Williams and Nat King Cole were early absorptions from this musical osmosis, then Elvis' *Hound Dog* which I used to ape performing on my first guitar, along with Conway Twitty in this rock'n'roll vein; the Beatles via Ed Sullivan and a yearning for something as provocative yet still disguised in suits and ties, and then deeply in Norfolk, hearing *Oh, Pretty Woman* by Roy Orbison that I still see potently in black and white to this day of writing. But my initial and significant purchases of actual recordings were 45s in Germany, 35 of them (yes, I have counted) which included, though I won't tally in their entirety, the eclectic range of The Kinks and their first three garage singles, Bobby Herb *Sunny*, The Marketts *Out of Limits*, The Platters *With this Ring*, that beautiful *Don't You Care* by The Buckinghams, the Shadows of Knight version of *Gloria* – the first song and chord sequence I learned, along with millions of others, two of the Beatles, three of The Mamas & the Pappas, Charlie Ryan *Hot Rod Lincoln* (absurdly), Nini Rosso *Der Clown*, Walter Wanderley *Call Me*, a gorgeous cover by The Silkie of *You've Got to Hide Your Love Away*, the rousing and parenthetically superfluous Blues Magoos *(We Ain't Got) Nothing Yet)*, The Impressions *I'm So Proud* which three black GIs spontaneously sang a cappella to my sister Melanie at the Karlsruhe outdoor swimming pool one summer's day, The Electric Prunes *I Had Too Much To Dream Last Night*: an original single that I recently sat on and cracked – so this and the catalyst for my one fist-fight beating, and finally the first 'heavy' song I ever heard that instilled a lifelong headbanger's addiction which came from that pulsing of the Music Machine's incendiary-for-its-time *Talk Talk*: all of this recalled and written as I listen to Black Sabbath's eponymous monument to Loud.

Making Sense of it all for a Friend

I liked the place where we went for a meal together, large
and quiet and light with proper chairs at a round table and
no music. We could talk. The food was wholesome, though
too much to eat for him, and I couldn't manage my second
beer. We talked of his travelling: spreading her ashes where
they had been together – so much for a petite person – like
how to dig a hole in sand at beaches, not throw to the wind.
I said I loved hearing her still answering the phone (her
recorded message) but he didn't know. *I never ring home*
he told me, which made sense, like later our hearing
nightingales sing.

Bio Siblings Release of Info

Section 43-124, Revised Statutes, as amended: "The Department of Health and Human Services Finance and Support shall provide a form which may be signed by a relative indicating the fact that such relative consents to his or her name being released to such relative's adopted person as provided by sections 43-113, 43-119 to 43-146, 71-626, 71-626.01, and 81-627.02. Such consent shall be effective as of the time of filing the form with the Department of Health and Human Services System, Finance and Support." I completed and submitted mine in 2005, the first search and the one still questing. I filled in the biological details and dates known, and signed, providing permission *to give your name and other information to the adopted person designated.* And it is in these prescriptions and designations that the form still rests, restless in its formality of indifference, or dormant as irony in its expression of a presumed future as well as strong assertion and intention: what shall be shall be.

Sung Worship

It was so welcomingly hot that July morning, sitting outside beneath the shade of a parasol with the fanning cool of breeze, reading the newspapers. Over the road, doors were open to the New Life Church who every Sunday worshipped there, weekend learners in the school's assembly hall, allowing air in and their pretty singing out, hymns which partly soothed the barbs of my absolute disdain for that benediction. They cheered too, whoops of winning and joy at a challenge being played, bonding within the psychology of such struggle and belief in their belonging. I thanked the summer's sun and our brief walk together before that shared serenade, the two of us having done our best with uncertainty that day.

Omaha, Nebraska: Just Mentioning List

For someone who couldn't wait to leave America – but not specifically Omaha, Nebraska where I was born – I have retained an attachment to the latter which is nonetheless peculiar considering the former. This is manifested in my collecting over the years references to both city and state in song, poetry, film and other occasional sources. Favourites from these, and not a complete account from my collection, are as follows – [1] a classic from two mentions of Nebraska in Lucia Berlin's short story 'A Manual for Cleaning Women': *"Yes," you said. A simple Nebraska statement*, [2] poets either born in, living in or closely connected to Nebraska (usually academia) and who have written directly about Omaha and/or the State: Stacey Waite; Marjorie Saiser; Shirley Buettner; Susan Aizenberg; Greg Kosmicki; Greg Kuzma; Michael Catherwood; Michael Skau; J.J. McKenna; Kevin Young; Martha Collins; Michael Anania; Jim Harrison; Erin Bilieu; Weldon Kees; Michael Dumanis; John D. Neihardt; Ted Kooser; Twyla Hansen; Clark Coolidge; Don Welch; Matt Mason; Lenora Castillo; William Kloefkorn; William Reichard; Billy Collins, [3] TV and/or film: from 'The West Wing'

BARTLET
I don't want to intimidate you, but it turns out I'm the first Democrat in twenty years to make a clean sweep of the Plains states and I'm not just talking about Iowa and Nebraska.

ABBEY
Are you trying to turn me on now?

ABBEY
All right;

a line from Little Bill Daggett in 'Unforgiven': *I heard that one myself, Bob. Hell, I even thought I was dead 'til I found out it was just that I was in Nebraska,* [4] songs with the title 'Omaha': the Everly Brothers, Waylon Jennings, Counting Crows, Walter Trout; songs that feature this city in the title: John Stewart 'Omaha Rainbow', Moby Grape 'Omaha Obtuse'; songs that feature the city in lyrics: Chris Smither 'Crocodile Man', Bob Dylan 'I Shall Be Free No. 10', C.W. McCall 'Convoy'; Preston Love's album titled 'OMAHA BAR-B-Q', and [5] quarterback Peyton Manning's use of 'Omaha': as an indicator word when taking the snap in football, and as described by the man himself *Well, 'Omaha', it's a run play. But it could be a pass play, or a play-action pass depending on a couple of things: the wind, which way we're playing, the quarter, and the jerseys that we're wearing,* which is presumably his idea of a joke, and the word has been used subsequently by many other QBs, presumably just for the same fun of it. I know Ginsberg mentions both Nebraska and Omaha in *Wichita Vortex Surta,* but going through all the references I have, and even the ones I don't yet could find, would be a nonsense whereas this selection of many is entirely reasonable.

Sibling Sections

I have 3 sisters + 1 + another, and perhaps 1 more. Tom and I are outnumbered by a combination of known and unknown numbers, which is arithmetic and discovery, or not, with the latter. Most of my life it has been Melanie, Julie and Patty, in that order, and we first lived all together, really, in Germany. Geography has controlled the relationships: Melanie and me are framed by Omaha and Elk Horn; Julie, Patty and me by Ipswich. As a family that travelled and lived in these partitions, this is how we grew up together – Melanie, for example, did not move to the UK in 1967. As I left my American limbo to return to its English destiny in 1970, our communal sections, when viewed over a lifetime, were relatively transient. Melanie, Julie and Patty eventually ended up together with Mom in the cosmopolitan town of Ashland, Oregon, and that was a blessing, especially for its comparative permanence. I met Bobbie Ann from a distance by email and Facebook in 2014, having found this side of the family a few years before, and I had one week getting to know her face-to-face when visiting Las Vegas in 2017. Bobbie Ann had discovered a new sister herself years earlier – *Stan the Ladies' Man* true to Lorraine's expectations – and though I do not know why, this is a connection I haven't pursued, nor she with me. There is the other sibling out there in the Unidentified, if with us still. Tom and I have therefore each inherited an extended family of at least four – Tom perhaps five; for me, who knows how many more have played Olin's guitar?

Afternoon Stroll and That White Ass

The mallards didn't give a proverbial, but the egret shat itself as I approached, an ironic ducks-and-drakes with feet dragging along the streamlet, always ahead until a final panic made it take flight away. What is it in our genealogy that casts us as brave or cowardly? I have only had two scraps – that first failed fist-fight with the boy who was a gentleman – so losing both, technically, when I ran from the next one without feeling a need to stay and help the others out. I'm no fox or plume hunter, so both species were safe. But my enemies were never on an afternoon stroll, and the years I have stood my ground are tougher than being attacked in an isolated alley or unlit street. Give me the fear in that surrender of a fleeing white ass – any day – over this unrelenting daily fight.

Complaining

The first 'letter' of complaint (it was written in Akkadian cuneiform) was apparently produced in 1750 BC from a customer Nanni to the merchant Ea-nasir who sold him poor quality metal ingots and was rude to the servant who had been sent to pay for and collect these. It is therefore an ancient as well as noble tradition, and writing this now I'm already composing in my head what I'll later write in my letter to Lidl about lunchtime's *Greek Style Pastitsio*. I'll point out the incongruency between package imagery showing a third of a layer of meat and the reality of that ingredient's virtual absence in what I had to eat. I know I'll also focus on the irony of another image which includes profile outlines of *both* a steer and a pig to further boast of the meaty recipe, as well as a product description which summarises a 'pasta dish layered with meat and béchamel sauce': no mention of the macaroni that is actually the main constituent foodstuff beneath the pottage. And I can already see myself working up to a linguistic frenzy in drawing a sarcastic observation from the etymological roots of the dish's name – and their pathetic representation of it – as *pastiche*. In the annals of my lifelong commitment to such missive missions, and continuing a criticising custom, this is going to be a doozy. It is worth adding, by the way, that I am a lifelong fan of Lidl and especially their *Greek Week* and similar special offers, so I will have suggestions for any recompense.

Luxtons in the Lane

There goes Young Luxton in his Massey Ferguson 565 and we both wave to one another, as always. He is, more accurately, *Old* Luxton – this being 30+ years since I'd be waving to his father riding by the same, as well as meet up once a month at his shop in town to pay for those milk deliveries, also so long gone. Their working every day (until one no more) is an ethic I've always admired, remember mine first learned on my two farms years ago and still going strong in its alternative patterns. It was at my second farm I drove a Massey Ferguson 185, the model before this one I've just seen, so also showing my age, and while I would be out in a field, he chugs by in the lane with a glorious calm and slow pace, always arriving in time for when it really doesn't matter more than being there, different to the young bucks I now watch racing by, like me back in former times and seeing others have to get out of the way.

Dreams

I have not said the ironic *good night* but mentioned my love and touched that watery blue glass on the bedroom wall which I dream will soothingly roll its wave on wave for her to also dream in real sleep. But as for the both of us, these are just that.

Not Going Back to School

Writing with Hammers is my only novel and it is all about my teaching experiences, based on many real people – students and teachers – as well as events that did happen. These are complemented by imaginary episodes and the tone is generally satirical in presenting the passion and fury of a career. I think my 'wisest' chapter was the one titled *Banned* which I wrote as an imagined episode but based on the actual experiences of regretting seeing teachers who had retired from the job returning to the school for casual visits, many quite regular. Although I liked meeting former colleagues and friends, I never had time to socialise with them, appearing as they did at short morning breaks and my having to leave mid-catching-up as the bell sounded for the next lesson. I decided not to make similar returns when I retired, and have stuck to this self-promise for over the last ten years. This is the chapter:

Banned

Members of staff at the school have banned retired teachers from returning to visit. It isn't that they come back to gloat or that their peace of mind and smooth skin are unintentional taunts that the rest of us find disturbing.

Before the ban, I speak to Jim who comes back after a few months to collect books of his that someone has found in his former classroom cupboard.

"It's good to see you. You're looking well," I tell him.

"I can't complain," he says.

"How do you spend your time?" I ask.

"This and that, as the saying goes," he says with a smile.

"I don't suppose you miss this place?"

"No."

"Is not working as great as they say?" I enquire.

"I've noticed that the moon rises in a different place each night," Jim replies.

He talks a little more about how waves don't pound, or drum or crash on the shore. He says they return applauding their rhythms. He tells me that if you follow a river far enough you will understand where it is coming from.

Jim never used to talk like this.

One day before the ban, Sandra also comes back to school just to say hello. She hasn't forgotten anything and no one has found any personal belongings that she has left behind. I speak to her as well.

"It's good to see you. You're looking happy," I tell her.

"I feel good," she says.

"Are you keeping busy?" I ask.

"There's always something to do," she replies.

"And you're having a good time?"

"Yesterday there were frozen droplets of dew on the escallonia leaves and they looked like thousands of tiny mirrors," she replies.

She talks about how when she touches these frozen water-pearls they drop to the ground as if from a broken necklace.

I speak to other staff about these conversations and they say they have had similar experiences. People say it is exactly the same when speaking with other teachers who have retired and return to school for whatever reason.

It isn't arranged specially, but at the next staff meeting we all have a vote and it is pretty unanimous that staff who have retired should be banned from returning to school. We all generally agree that there isn't time to have such conversations. It is also considered preferable to let them go gracefully and to find their own feet, so to speak.

Tree Feller

With a billhook and a pruning saw I took down the tree, an ash not fully grown, obviously, but enough to be sweaty work on a frosty day. The hook was over forty years old in my possession, and me sixty-two trying to be the young man I was back then, but the racing heart and rests in the patio chair put that ambition to shame. I had a chain saw but it was still boxed after many years, too afraid to try and swing the same as I did when wooding on the farm. That morning was not as reckless as the last time I tackled the tree, falling down the ladder and holding on to rip muscles in my arm, soothed with pain-killers for some time afterwards until another ache refrained. This day was well prepared with rope and props and calculations for the cut, stopping to survey instead of running ahead, and in the end it fell exactly where I had planned and not reduced the rhododendron to mush or swiped me across the back, dead. I'd have to keep an eye on the stump as ash grows back quickly, long young shoots I might have allowed to try and then severed to weave in another rustic fence. It was a cycle, and I survived, so far, like not tumbling from the high hedges too, all this existential gardening with a look to being more careful with a swung hook, but a trimmer cord was cut to its death by circuit breakers that saved and protected me, still life in this older feller yet.

Our House

Returning from the sunshine mall of seventies Laurel
Canyon, Graham Nash wrote *Our House* for Joni, himself
and me in one happy hour – a melody of peace and love and
other imaginings moving through the piano keys – and I
returned home from our small-time shopping spree to pen
some lines, willing enough when singing along, but then
way beyond those dreams, and this is our song: I'll light a
fire to keep the cold from her malady and bring flowers too
to place in a vase she made years before when life would
never seem so hard, and the evening sunshine could be a
real dream of summer when I will mow the moss and weeds
of our yard whilst humming old songs like a noise in the
breeze.

Sunflowers

Pulling the sunflowers from the ground was accepting an ending, but they were all past flowering apart from one or two small Teddy Bear bursts of sun, though clearly also dying out. If there were any seeds, nature would take its course, and that would be those remaining after the two visits from the goldfinch and his colourful acrobatic feasting when perched on top and pecking them out from upside down. It was the music I didn't understand, a choral-like pastoral seeming in the background but emanating from the raised beds along which the sunflowers had been planted and staked. Even bashing the dirt out from their pulled roots on the wooden surround didn't drown out the sound, but rather added a dulled thud of a beat. And it wasn't the radio from my neighbour's house and instead the resonating bees who were also after finales in the last nectar of the lavender there, no more or less a surprise than anything else on that day.

Close Reach

Tom sent me his framed picture of the prone shape of a body, left leg angled, head concealed by an open door, arms raised to the reach of fluorescent lights, and a gesture of query or euphoria from its expectant position. Whether comic metaphor, light borrowed because it was needed, or composition found in its moment, the silver lining to its share has become our corresponding and learning: as a brotherly game of tag, this is now our ongoing journey after all those years. When re-reading his email communiqués and letters, I continue to discover their poetic depths and wisdom, ponder the nature/nurture argument of our link and lineage, and wonder at the hopefulness of inheritance in shared maternal genes, or marvel at the fortuity in such apparent symbiosis. In one black and white photo he also sent, Tom searches through a Nikon, looking, and I'm there watching and waiting to be seen. It is now well over a year since meeting and we haven't yet used technology, apart from those written electronic exchanges, as well as images, and it seems we are steeped in the comfort but also mystique of a familiarity born of age and habit. Or just our words. His pull their derivations from jazz and Laurel Canyon, the technological in photography, esoterica (for me) of Thornton Wilder as well as the *Hot Rod*, and a deep well of love, generosity and forgiveness. I suspect he has conveyed as completely as this long before I became anywhere near to it.

My brother Tom

Walking at Jacob's Ladder, Sidmouth

Stones had crept up the beach steps but they never made it all the way – no tidal of skimming stones could propel pebbles beyond the sand and water of their belonging. Even wishful thinking climbed just so far before real hands and shovels would come to scoop them back, not *like* but totally *as* the rock they were. It was the same in that way earth is never linked to a heaven no matter how people dream and however their babel tries to confuse and persuade. Take a stone and put it in your hand and feel the cold but rounded reality. After millions of years and the crashing of waves these would be the dust of the earth, stuff that comes and goes but is not walking out of water to ascend these stairs. Out to sea and somewhere in this charcoal share of sky and shore, a winter bather approached curls of waves in the hope these would furl upwards – another hopefulness – up from darkness to light even though grey, from the cold to a different cold that warmed because it had been swum, reached with strokes like those that brush-stroked this scene in some dark swimmer's imaginings. The horizon was not black but black lines pivoted under the waves, stepped outwards under the froth. Without colour who knows anything other than what is made of shade, unless in their doubting there is the wader's fear of drowning. And back onshore where the buildings were, how the stone greys, cement sames, pebble hues, sand, sea seeps, oxidation, rust-bled lines from former attachments long severed, and all the shades of debris dumped in the ocean over years and years, had risen to pretty pastels along the beach-hut fronts, numbered doors noting who lived here and in the now of their paint-strokes. How many had carved a name or obscenity at low tide – it *would* be washed away – as we knew from scribes who had etched history in its otter sandstone along the low cliff faces (mercia mud too high unless it is falling on that longhand) over time? Questions of osmosis absorbed in the moment; someone opened a baby-blue one to wave goodbye at another outside.

Where We Stood

A friend and I meet up by chance every month or so when both out walking in Ottery at the same time, perhaps shopping for food, and on one of these kinds of days we were standing where *Kubla Khan* begins, Coleridge's paradise poem along the Land of Canaan footpath and its walking promise, putting our world to rights as an election was coming – rueing how a disenfranchised would still vote for the privileged and liars: this incongruent opium of imagining and hope – and the dog-poo bin was also next to us reeking each time a good citizen passed by and opened it to deposit their black bag of ad nauseam.

Snowflakes

In marking exam papers, especially over three and a half decades, I have read many interesting things written not as answers to questions, but for example as complaints or pleas or completely random asides to the examiner, so when something genuinely surprising comes along I would make a note to myself, for instance with this line *even if the life is cruel* which was a final sentence written on its own at the top of an otherwise empty concluding page from the student's Answer booklet. I noticed it working up through the script online from that last page, clerically marking pages as 'seen' ready for that other marking to follow when judging chronologically what had led to this apocalypse. Assuming the writer had responded to all preceding it, I knew this was a reference to Michael Laskey's poem *Nobody*, the unseen for that year and a poem about taking a chance in living, so I hoped – at the age of sixteen – the young person would in their life look for the snow to tread and mess about in, throw a big round one at nobody in particular, and laugh at the cruelty that might one day be.

Autumn Poems

There's an English professor I know who wrote a brief critical review of a great writer's latest work, a poet clearly admired and adored for a previous output, but in this latest book, written aged 89, he is censured for continually rehashing clichés on old age and dying, using a wilting lexis that moved shakily with meanings, reminding – reminding – if we can imagine, how pacing to the end is a slow dread of the inevitable, one of many walked before. And *dread of* could be *trudge to*, though when you are past it, others will have to be the judge. It made me think that if out of routine I ever write another 'autumnal' poem – and I've done a few, even using that word – I hope I'll immediately destroy it. I'm not talking about the weather, but metaphors used as dry and dead as falling leaves...and there I go again, forgetful, falling back into the old deadener of habit.

Names

At the seafront where we would, as usual, collectively cross paths – Handbag Lady, Stomach Man, Mustachio Guy and That Nice Couple – it was an uncommon day when only Stomach Man was walking the promenade with us (That Nice Couple) though we did see a newbie I will name Pyjama Person strolling along the road running adjacent, yet I assumed this was a one-off rather than a usual there where I have established names for so many of the regulars at this geriatric seaside town that can make us feel young: that is until local elderlies romp by us with our walker which probably prompts our designating endearment, although we have never heard it said out loud – not in the way I turned to her and audibly announced, for example, when Handbag Lady was strolling towards us, swinging it from her left hand in great long arcs to match the stride, or Mustachio Guy with his tweed and brogues and designer sunglasses. Stomach Man's legs are tendrils so this accentuates his belly, but that day he was wearing a dark weather-breaker smock so you would have to know what his physical specialism was on most other, regular days.

Tree Bark

This is the *tree bark* moment – whether to treat it figuratively even though cicadas did once cling and leave their shells as actual memory, or find it in its many names of explaining. I've been waiting years to do this, stripping away at the ideas to leave just the playful behind, but now with all those words, there is a pre-meditation as reckoning. So, I'll spit it out: how the *phloem* is comically the sound of a pun yet also the first layer of meaning – sugary in all aspects of what it feeds. Then there is that further choice, whether it is *xylem* or *sapwood*, and I'll go for the latter to make it appear like empathy rather than a science. Yet already I'm done on this construction, unwilling to go to the *cambium* and its trajectory. Rather, it is back to layers, and in this life it is with their dark depths as wraparound and enclosure; that hard shell where as tissue it's not nature or art but constriction like a dead wood sheath, harder than looking for the signals of an ending it won't allow us to make.

Forty-Two Years on the Job

She had of late bought calming bracelet beads and healing stones which I didn't mind if helping because I do believe in the power of positive thinking – even hope – as well as desperation. And although so unlikely, I didn't want her looking for gods, especially that one with the obnoxious story of suffering and reward, a telling I have seethed to over these forty-two years like a perverse occupation.

Two Grey Beards

The grey-bearded man walking towards me looked like a long-lost twin there on holiday above Marton in the South Lakes where wind turbines crooned to the sheep. We stopped and said hello and were soon talking about oil barons and political shenanigans and how the turbines were ugly objects – wave power the better alternative but not with petroleum in the ground and those men who run things still so full of desire. On this we agreed, and it was amazing how quickly a conversation developed, he suggesting I take a walk at Pennington assuming I was as committed as him, and it seemed right to explain a problem when I told him of my wife's infirmity. He asked outright and I informed him of the forty years and he praised her for doing so well, when I agreed, again. The turbines still turned, sheep ignoring the whirr and moving shadows. We both looked out beyond where we stood and a lamb bleated for its mother, lost for a few seconds. I had earlier taken pictures of the turbines on green hills against blue skies and all those sheep grazing at their sides. I wanted to suggest there was a beauty in those contrasts, but thought better of it. One picture I saw later when viewing on the camera's screen was a city of wind machines in the haze out at sea we both commented on when talking, he not knowing of my collection of ugly things made beautiful in their surroundings. Where we might have concurred more if discussing this, is how in life we make the best of things, even if a fleeting spin on a country lane with two grey-bearded men.

Survival and Surrender

I wanted her sitting next to me driving home with the top down on a balmy, early summer evening, warmed also by the night's jazz – that one about survival and surrender with a trumpeter's lyrical shift to the squeal of how a struggle for freedom is spiritual without our believing in it.

Printed in Great Britain
by Amazon